# NOLO *Your Legal Companion*

W9-BPP-092

*"In Nolo you can trust."* —**THE NEW YORK TIMES**

Whether you have a simple question or a complex problem, turn to us at:

## NOLO.COM
### Your all-in-one legal resource
Need quick information about wills, patents, adoptions, starting a business—or anything else that's affected by the law? **Nolo.com** is packed with free articles, legal updates, resources and a complete catalog of our books and software.

## NOLO NOW
### Make your legal documents online
Creating a legal document has never been easier or more cost-effective! Featuring Nolo's Online Will, as well as online forms for LLC formation, incorporation, divorce, name change—and many more! Check it out at **http://nolonow.nolo.com**.

## NOLO'S LAWYER DIRECTORY
### Meet your new attorney
If you want advice from a qualified attorney, turn to Nolo's Lawyer Directory—the only directory that lets you see hundreds of in-depth attorney profiles so you can pick the one that's right for you. Find it at **http://lawyers.nolo.com**.

## ALWAYS UP TO DATE
### Sign up for NOLO'S LEGAL UPDATER
Old law is bad law. We'll email you when we publish an updated edition of this book—sign up for this free service at nolo.com/legalupdater.

### Find the latest updates at NOLO.COM
Recognizing that the law can change even before you use this book, we post legal updates during the life of this edition at **nolo.com/updates**.

### Is this edition the newest? ASK US!
To make sure that this is the most recent edition available, just give us a call at **800-728-3555**.

(Please note that we cannot offer legal advice.)

YOUR
LITTLE Legal
Companion

by the Editors of Nolo

NOLO

First Edition      MAY 2006
Cover & Book Design      SUSAN PUTNEY
Proofreading      JOE SADUSKY
Printing      DELTA PRINTING SOLUTIONS, INC.

Your little legal companion : helpful advice for life's big events / from the editors of Nolo.
     p. cm.
     ISBN 1-4133-0542-3
     1. Law--United States--Outlines, syllabi, etc. 2. Law--United States--Popular works. 3.
Life skills--United States--Outlines, syllabi, etc. 4. Life skills--United States--Popular
works. I. Nolo (Firm)
     KF387.L58 2006
     646.7--dc22

2006043785

Quantity sales: For information on bulk purchases or corporate premium sales, please
contact the Special Sales department. For academic sales or textbook adoptions, ask
for Academic Sales, 800-955-4775. Nolo, 950 Parker St., Berkeley, CA 94710.

We believe accurate, plain-English legal information should help you solve many of
your own legal problems. But this text is not a substitute for personalized advice from
a knowledgeable lawyer. If you want the help of a trained professional—and we'll
always point out situations in which we think that's a good idea—consult an attorney
licensed to practice in your state.

## About the Authors

Every Nolo project is collaborative—but this one was truly a group effort. All of Nolo's legal editors wrote parts of the book, and we had some fun doing it. But greatest credit is due to **Tamara Traeder**, who came up with many of the ideas for this book, put everything together, gave it just the right tone, and did it cheerfully and well.

# Table of Contents

# Let Freedom Ring

## Going to College

Are you experiencing the joy (and terror) of leaving home and going to school? You won't believe how much you're going to learn, both in class and out. Here are some things to keep in mind as you get started.

**TEN**
things you
should know

1 **Act out.** It's tough to leave home, especially if you're leaving a nice one. That's why, during your last year of high school, you need to get really unpleasant—so everyone (including you) can feel relieved, not sad, when you go.

2 **What if I'm a geek?** Your roommate is as worried about meeting you as you are about him. Most of the time, your toys will be as cool and up-to-date as his.

3 **It's never too late to grow up.** You'll be amazed at how much your parents have matured in the short time between your leaving for college and Thanksgiving.

4 **No shame in getting help.** If you find that college is way harder than high school, chances are your high school didn't prepare you for this level of work. Consider getting some tutoring.

5 **They can't do that—can they?** Unfortunately, the Fourth Amendment, which protects us against most unannounced searches and seizures, hasn't made it into your RA's rule book. An uninvited visit to check for beer in the fridge is probably okay.

6 **You'll find your tribe.** Science majors often become clearer thinkers than English majors. However, English majors may catch up when they inevitably enter law school (what else can they do?). Where do you fit?

Your Little Legal Companion

**7**   **The credit wave.** You'll be bombarded with credit card offers. Don't fall for them—it's really easy to get out of control. (You may already be out of control in other ways, but we won't address that here.)

**8**   **You really are a grownup.** Most colleges won't discuss your grades or your health with your parents. That could be a blessing, or it could be a problem. Either way, you are en route to being on your own.

**9**   **Make connections.** A personal relationship with a teacher who will write you a thoughtful letter of recommendation is worth at least two-tenths of a grade point.

**10**   **Now for the important stuff.** You can date your roommate's steady, skip every class but the final, and borrow every book—but never, ever, wash your darks with your lights.

*Don't waste time in college* taking staid courses like history and math when you have these classes available:

- "Philosophy and Star Trek" at Georgetown University.

- "The Art of Sin and the Sin of Art" at Rhode Island School of Design (the catalog promises that you'll "lust with the saints and burn with the sinners").

- "Daytime Serials: Family and Social Roles" at the University of Wisconsin.

- "From Pot to Pills: Exploring the World of Recreational Drugs," offered at the University of California, Santa Barbara.

# Welcome to 9-5

**2**

## Your First Job

Whether your first spoken words on the job are "Do you want fries with that?" or "I represent the plaintiff," there are a few things you should know before your first work experience begins.

**TEN**
things you
should know

1  **Don't lie to get a job.** If you can't do the work, both you and your boss will be unhappy. And plenty of companies will fire you for lying on your application or resume.

2  **Bring your ID.** Your new employer has to verify that you're legally eligible to work in the U.S., which means you'll need to bring a passport, citizenship or naturalization certificate, green card, or some combination of other documents proving your identity and work status.

3  **Don't expect free health insurance.** Employers aren't required to provide it. Fewer than two-thirds of private employers make health insurance available, and most of them require employees to foot part of the bill.

4  **No one owes you paid vacation, holidays, or sick time.** No law requires companies to offer these benefits, and some of them don't. Those that do are free to impose certain eligibility rules—for example, you can't take any vacation until you've worked there for six months.

5  **Get ready to sign on the dotted line.** Many companies get the work relationship off to a warm and fuzzy start by asking new employees to sign an "at-will agreement," stating that they can be fired at any time, for any legal reason. (In case you're planning to protest, they can also fire you for refusing to sign the form.)

**6** **Stand up for yourself.** Many new employees—particularly teenagers working in retail and food service jobs—are mistreated by supervisors who assume that they don't know their rights. If you are sexually harassed, forced to work off the clock, or exposed to safety hazards, speak up.

**7** **Make yourself useful.** Take on as many new responsibilities as you can, and try to work for different supervisors. Not only will you quickly learn what you are good at, you'll also create allies and make yourself more valuable to the company—the best job insurance around.

**8** **Don't be a know-it-all.** One of the biggest complaints employers have about hiring recent college graduates is that they have an inflated sense of themselves.

**9** **Try to fit in.** Let your work—not the way you dress or express yourself—stand out. There will be plenty of time for personal fashion statements when you own your own company.

**10** **It's all about who you know.** Make connections with your coworkers and supervisors, and stay in touch with them even if you leave this job. The best job opportunities come from personal contacts, not from the want ads.

## Match the Celebrity to His or Her First Job

(1) Stephen King     (a) Recalibrated car odometers

(2) Demi Moore     (b) Worked as a school janitor

(3) Christopher Walken     (c) Worked for a debt collection agency

(4) Jay Leno     (d) Photographed naked for a calendar

(answers: 1 is b, 2 is c, 3 is d, 4 is a.)

# Your Very Own Wheels

**3**

## Buying a Car

Shopping for a new ride is a whole lot different from what it used to be. As a buyer, you have more options and much greater access to information.

**TEN**
things you
should know

**1**   **Surf to ride.** Use websites such as kbb.com (Kelly Blue Book), edmunds.com, and nadaguides.com (National Auto Dealer Association) to check out makes, models, gas mileage, optional features, and colors. Investigate financing sources, evaluate your warranty options, and get an insurance quote—all before you step out the door.

**2**   **It adds up.** Don't forget sales tax, typical service costs for your model, and ongoing registration and insurance costs when figuring out what you can afford.

**3**   **History matters.** If you've found the right used car, buy a vehicle history report from carfax.com or autocheck.com to alert you to inspections, repairs, accidents, floods, possible odometer rollbacks, and other need-to-know events in the car's history. You'll need the vehicle identification number (VIN) to do so.

**4**   **Keep quiet and stay firm.** Don't let the seller know how much you have to spend, the details of your financing, or how badly you need a new car. You know what you want, and how much you'll pay. Stick with your plan. Be ready to walk away.

**5**   **Hate negotiation?** Consider buying through membership clubs such as AAA or Costco, or at used car "superstores." You can also hire an auto broker to do the negotiating for you. Ask around.

**6** **Be safe.** If you're looking at cars listed in the classifieds or on the Internet, don't go alone to see a car or get in one, and meet in a public, well-lit place.

**7** **Should you buy a warranty?** Buying an extended warranty for a new or used car sounds great, but it could be disastrous if the warranty company goes belly-up. Research the warranty company at bbb.org (Better Business Bureau) before signing the contract.

**8** **Don't sign blindly.** Don't feel pressured to sign any contract right away. Take the documents home and read them carefully. If you're not comfortable, have someone else read them, too.

**9** **Buying used?** Used car dealers generally must display a Buyer's Guide on the car. Any differences you negotiate with the seller must be reflected on the Buyer's Guide—it decides future disagreements with the seller, even if you negotiated something else. If the "As-Is" box is checked, future repairs are up to you.

**10** **Keep it in the family?** Before buying a car from a friend or relative, consider the effect on your relationship if the car dies and the seller chooses not to take responsibility.

Buying a Car    3

## *Did you hear that?*

Want to know what that noise is coming from under the hood of your car or the back wheel? NPR's Click and Clack can help. Their online Car Talk Car Noise Emporium has 30 different car noises—from "vubb, vubububub, vubb, vubububub" to "who, whu, wuuu, wuuu." Simply click on the part of the car where you hear the noise, find the sound you're hearing, and read the official diagnosis.

## *A vote of confidence*

40% of Americans say that used-car salesmen are generally more ethical than members of Congress.

# Home Sweet Home

4

## Renting an Apartment

Renting your home is an odd mix of personal and business considerations—personal for you and business for the landlord. Before choosing a place and signing a lease, you should know some of what your landlord knows.

**TEN**
things you
should know
• • • • • • • • • ▶

1   **New paint is not a constitutional right.** Landlords don't have to repaint before you move in (except in New York City, and there it's required only every three years).

2   **Everybody's memory fades, even yours.** Get your rental deal in writing, including the rent, deposits, and other key terms of the deal. If the landlord agreed to fumigate the closet, put it in the lease.

3   **"But I'm sure you said . . . ."** If you don't put your agreement in writing, but agree orally, you're still bound to the deal for up to one year. It's just going to be harder to convince someone—like a judge or jury—that your version is the true one.

4   **Think again about those tap dancing lessons.** One man's ceiling is another man's floor. If you're an inconsiderate neighbor, your landlord has legal grounds to kick you out.

5   **Don't end up paying for damage that was already there.** Walk through the rental with the landlord, a clipboard, and a digital camera that will date-stamp its pictures and document the condition of the place. Ask the landlord to sign off on your notes (if he won't, at least you have pictures).

6   **Hospitality is golden—but not to your landlord.** A long-term guest looks like an unauthorized occupant to a landlord—and it's grounds for terminating your tenancy. When your guest

starts receiving mail at your place, it's time to notify the landlord and ask to add your new roomie to the lease.

**7** **Taste does not matter.** No matter how much you hate your heliotrope bedroom, never repaint without the landlord's consent. You could end up paying a painter to reapply that lovely hue.

**8** **Hold your fire.** Don't withhold the rent when your landlord refuses to make repairs unless you're sure your state allows it and you're doing it for a big-deal problem.

**9** **Get renters' insurance.** Your landlord's property insurance won't cover your belongings if they're lost in a fire or burglary, or damaged by that overflowing bathtub upstairs.

**10** **When you must break a lease.** In most states you're not automatically responsible for the remaining rent under the lease. The landlord has to take reasonable steps to rerent and credit what you owe with the new tenant's rent. This also means that he can't just pocket the entire security deposit as a penalty for leaving early.

Renting an Apartment **4**

## You really mean that?

Excerpts from actual letters sent to landlords:

- The toilet is blocked and we cannot bathe the children until it is cleared.

- This is to let you know that there is a smell coming from the man next door.

- The toilet seat is cracked: Where do I stand?

- I request your permission to remove my drawers in the kitchen.

- Our lavatory seat is broken in half and is now in three pieces.

- Our kitchen floor is very damp, we have two children and would like a third, so will you please send someone to do something about it.

- Could you please send someone to fix our bath tap? My wife got her toe stuck in it and it is very uncomfortable for us.

# Sharing Spaces

**5**

## Choosing a Roommate

Sharing a lease, refrigerator, and bathroom
with someone you know and love can be
challenging. Try doing it with a stranger.
When considering possible roommates, even
those you think you know well, think about
the following.

1   **Opposites may make great friends, but not necessarily great roommates.** That cool chick who "brings out your wild side" may not be the best choice as your roommate if you are normally quiet and introspective. Be completely honest: Do you share a passion for neatness? Is one of you a night owl? A smoker? Make sure your lifestyles are compatible.

2   **Would you loan this person the monthly rent?** If your roommate can't pay his share of the rent, you'll have to cover it or face eviction.

3   **Your roommate's screw-ups can cost you your tenancy.** The landlord can evict all of you for the wild party your buddy held last weekend, even though you were out of town.

4   **Be nice to your parents.** Landlords often ask student renters if their parents will cosign the lease, meaning the landlord can demand rent from the parents if the tenants don't pay. If one set of parents cosigns a lease, all parents should, so no one is stuck paying rent for someone else's kid.

5   **"Who moved my cheese?"** is not just a popular book. It could also be a troubling verbatim comment out of your roommate's mouth. Find out about your roommate's obsession with food and other quirks before you move in, by checking with her past roommates. Give her the opportunity to check out your bizarre habits, too.

**6**  **Have a frank discussion about overnight guests.**
A girlfriend who becomes a nightly fixture may as well be a
tenant—but she's not paying rent. Worse, you could get evicted
for having an unauthorized occupant (someone not screened and
approved by the landlord like you were).

**7**  **Create a system for splitting and paying bills, such as
electricity, phone, and cable.** If you're writing checks for shared
bills, make sure the other roommates pay you before the bills are
due. Otherwise, you guessed it—you're fronting another loan.

**8**  **Agree what will happen if someone wants to leave.** How
much notice will that roommate give the others? Will the departing
tenant be responsible for finding an acceptable replacement?

**9**  **Prepare for a breakup—what if some of you want a
roommate to leave?** (If couples can anticipate the end with a
prenuptial agreement, you can, too.) Consider agreeing to use a
landlord/tenant mediation service, which you'll find free in many
cities.

**10**  **When you move out,** the landlord will use your deposit to pay
for damage and needed cleaning, and he won't care a bit about
which roommate was responsible. It's up to you to apportion the
responsibility—and divide the returned deposit among yourselves
accordingly.

## Famous Roommates

- Bert and Ernie (*Sesame Street*)

- Oscar and Felix (*The Odd Couple*)

- Chandler and Joey (*Friends*)

- Al Gore and Tommy Lee Jones

- Gene Hackman and Al Pacino

- Gwyneth Paltrow and Winona Ryder

- Ben Affleck and Matt Damon

- Lindsay Lohan and Raven Simone

- Danny DeVito and Michael Douglas

- Dustin Hoffman and Robert Duvall

- Marilyn Monroe and Shelley Winters

# Doesn't Everyone Need One?

6

## Bringing That Adorable Puppy Home

Only someone with a heart of stone can resist a cuddly puppy—it's nature's way of finding them homes.

**TEN**
things you
should know

• • • • • • • • • ▶

1 **Never buy a dog from a pet store.** These poor pups are expensive, were probably raised under appalling conditions in a "puppy mill," and may be ill because they were shipped across the country at an early age.

2 **If you already did.** If you bought a dog from a pet store, and it turns out to be sick, you can get your money back if your state has a "lemon law" for dogs and you act quickly.

3 **Is that an HMO or PPO?** You can buy health insurance for your dog, but it's expensive. Then again, so is modern veterinary care. (Did you know your dog might get a CAT scan? So humiliating.)

4 **"But I like my dog better than my husband."** No matter how wonderful your dog is, you can't leave money to pets in your will.

5 **There is a solution.** In about half the states, you can set up a trust for your dog, naming a trustee to spend money you leave for the dog's benefit. But it's usually fine just to leave the dog (and some kibble money) to someone who agrees to take loving care of your dog if you can't.

6 **No special privileges.** It's legal for landlords to discriminate against pet owners by banning pets or charging a bigger security deposit. The only exceptions: trained service dogs that help owners living with disabilities.

**7** **All over the map.** Some airlines no longer accept dogs on flights. Others are relaxing some restrictions. Check with your carrier before a trip. Keep in mind, however, that flying can be risky for dogs.

**8** **Train and socialize your dog pronto.**
If your dog bites someone without provocation, you're probably going to be liable for the injured person's medical bills and lost income—and if the bite is serious, therapy bills. If it happens again, the consequences may be worse: a court could declare your dog dangerous or vicious and make you buy expensive liability insurance, a tall fence—and a muzzle.

*Ratio of humans to dogs regularly in Nolo's editorial offices: 15:3*

**9** **Don't be a nuisance.** If your dog turns out to be a barker (dogs left alone all day are often the worst offenders), you'll not only be very unpopular with your neighbors, you'll also risk being sued for, well, being a nuisance.

**10** **Dogs are great.** At least one study found that kids raised with a family dog score higher on self-esteem tests than do kids who grew up dog-deprived. Another study indicates that dog ownership helps lower blood pressure. Why else would we let dogs roam our editorial department?

*The law is a dull dog.*

**—Charles Dickens**

# Meet the Tax Man

## 7

## Filing Your First Federal Tax Return

Filing a tax return for the first time may seem daunting. You're right! However, after you've filed returns for about 20 years or so, it will be a snap. We've listed a few tips to get you started.

TEN
things you
should know

1 **Procrastinate, with IRS approval.** If you can't file your tax return by April 15, get a four-month extension by filing IRS Form 4868. However, you do need to file the form and pay any estimated taxes you owe by April 15 to avoid a penalty.

2 **All those wasted trees.** Recycle those paper 1040 forms from the IRS. For a few dollars, you can file online with TurboTax (Intuit) or TaxCut (H&R Block), which will walk you through your return.

3 **If you can't beat 'em, pay 'em.** Tempted to rebel? The IRS is nothing if not patient and persistent. If you cheat or choose not to pay taxes, you risk suffering the consequences. They aren't pretty.

4 **Start early.** As you begin receiving W-2s, 1099s, and other tax-related docs in January, stick them all into one folder so you'll have them handy for your return.

5 **Do you itemize?** Certain expenses such as home mortgage interest can be deducted from your income before calculating taxes. Or, you can choose to use the "standard" deduction—more than two-thirds of taxpayers do. Your tax program will do a quick calculation for you to see which results in paying lower taxes.

6 **Don't forget your education.** You may be able to take deductions for student loan interest (up to $2,500) or for tuition-related expenses (up to $4,000). Or you may be eligible for tax credits (the Hope Credit of up to $1,500 or the Lifetime

Learning Credit of up to $2,500) for courses you or a dependent took during the tax year. Each credit and deduction has different requirements, and all of them phase out depending on your income. See Publication 970 at www.irs.gov to get the nitty-gritty details.

7 **Clean out those closets.** Deductions for charitable contributions under $250 are rarely questioned, although you should save receipts. Take advantage of this tax break every year by taking a few boxes to Goodwill or Salvation Army.

8 **Use retirement accounts now.** Lower your income tax and rack up dollars towards your retirement. If your employer offers a 401(k), maximize your contributions, especially if your employer matches them. If not, open an IRA or a Roth IRA.

9 **Don't panic.** If you owe more taxes than you can pay, you can request an installment plan. Call the IRS at 800-829-1040 or file Form 9465 to request one. You'll pay interest and penalty charges for delaying payments, so pay as much tax as possible with your return.

10 **There's your state, too.** Unless you live in one of the following states, you'll need to file a tax return in the state in which you reside as well: Alaska, Florida, Nevada, South Dakota, Texas, Washington, and Wyoming. (New Hampshire taxes only interest and dividends.)

## How long do I have to keep my tax records?

Although the IRS recommends keeping records for three to seven years, there is no time limit for the IRS to audit what it thinks is a fraudulent return. See IRS Publication 552. We recommend keeping all of your returns and essential backup. Annoying, but you'll be glad to have them if an auditor comes knocking.

# I Didn't See Them Coming

**8**

## When You've Had a Car Accident

You're driving along, minding your own business, and wham! At best, you're feeling a rush of adrenaline and maybe a bit of shock. If you get into an accident, there are a few things to remember.

**TEN**
things you
should know

1 **Need we say this?** Don't just drive away (some people do). Check for injuries, then call 911 and ask what to do. Move your car? Wait for police? Ask the operator how to document the accident if police are not dispatched (you may need a police report later). Exchange license plate numbers and contact and insurance information with other involved drivers.

2 **Insult to injury.** If the other party was at fault and doesn't have insurance, get their contact information anyway. If you can't collect from your own insurance company, you may be able to sue the other driver in small claims or regular court.

3 **Accident report?** Check with your insurance company or your department of motor vehicles (DMV) to see if you are required to file one with the DMV.

4 **Take notes.** Write down all the circumstances of the accident and the effects of any injuries—large or small.

5 **Who's at fault?** The person who was careless or violated traffic laws. If you were partially at fault but the other driver was more careless, you may still be paid a percentage of your damages based on relative blame.

6 **What's the magic number?** Insurance adjusters calculate what to pay by adding up vehicle damage, medical expenses, and lost wages, then using a multiplier to account for pain and

suffering. Minor accidents get a multiplier of 1.5 or 2; serious accidents get a multiplier of 5 or more. The resulting number is the insurance company's starting point in negotiating a settlement.

7 **Heads up.** You or your insurance company must notify people in writing before filing a claim with their insurance companies. Any claim should then be filed immediately, stating the facts of the accident, the value of your losses, and evidence of pain and suffering.

8 **Don't be chatty.** If the other party's insurance company calls you before submitting your claim, take the name of the person calling, the insurance company he or she represents, and the insured; give limited personal information; refuse politely to discuss the accident or your injuries (just say you'll be filing a claim); resist any pressure to settle immediately; and set limits on future phone contact.

9 **None of their business.** The settlement amount should not deduct any amounts covered by your own health insurer or any paid time off you may have enjoyed. However, your own health insurance provider may require you to reimburse it out of any settlement.

10 **The awful truth.** We hate to say it, but … you may need a lawyer. If your injury was severe or resulted in a long-term or permanent disability, or if the insurance company refuses to pay, find an experienced personal injury lawyer.

When You've Had a Car Accident 8

*If you carry a cell phone,* program personal information and an emergency contact's name and phone numbers into your phone address book under "In Case of Emergency" or "ICE." Police, firefighters, emergency medical technicians, and emergency room staff are now trained to look in cell phones for this information.

# Take This Job and Shove It

**9**

## Quitting Your Job

You're going back to school. You got a better offer. For whatever reason, you're moving on …

TEN
things you
should know

• • • • • • • • • ▶

1 **It's only fair.** Give your employer at least two weeks' notice unless you have a very good reason—for example, you have a family emergency or your job is unsafe.

2 **Get a written letter of reference.** If you later lose touch with your supervisor, you still have a reference you can give prospective employers.

3 **Do a little research.** Many people leave their jobs without understanding what benefits continue even after their last day. Check out what you're entitled to: health insurance continuation (called COBRA), the money in a 401(k) or other retirement plan, stock options, and so on. You'll need to take some steps to protect these benefits, so check your employee handbook or talk to the human resources administrator.

4 **Tough duty.** In many states, you forfeit accrued vacation time when you quit. You may want to go ahead and take your vacation before giving notice.

5 **Getting paid.** If you don't get your final paycheck on your last day, contact your state's labor department to find out when your employer must give it to you.

6 **Keep your mouth shut (and we mean that in the nicest possible way).** When you are interviewing for a new job or after you've left, don't tell lies, gossip, or spread nasty rumors about your former boss or employer. It always gets back. At best, you will

have destroyed any future business relationships; at worst, you could be sued for defamation. And employers don't like to hire people who trash-talk about former workplaces.

**7** **The only exception to No. 6.** If you're quitting because of harassment, let your employer know ahead of time and give them a reasonable opportunity to correct the problem. If you don't give the company a chance to address it, you can't later sue for harassment.

**8** **Take care of yourself.** If money is tight, don't quit before knowing how you'll take care of yourself financially. Get information about public assistance and postponing or decreasing student loan or monthly credit card payments.

**9** **Stay in touch.** Make sure your company has your current contact information and knows not to give people your forwarding information unless you say it's okay.

**10** **Don't go off in a huff.** If your coworkers or supervisor want to take you out to lunch or after-work drinks, accept with good grace. You never know when you'll meet again.

## Movie Night

If you're bored with your job or considering a career change, take a gander at *Fast, Cheap & Out of Control*. The documentary profiles four men with unusual animal-related jobs: a lion tamer, a topiary gardener, a man who studies mole rats, and an MIT scientist who has designed insect-like robots.

Need a reminder that your office job isn't so bad after all? *Office Space* will introduce you to a boss even worse than your own. Then watch *9 to 5* to see an annoying boss get his comeuppance.

# You're Outta Here!

## Getting Fired

Seems like everyone wants to be The Donald these days. There are a few things you should know if you get called into the big office and told, "You're fired!"

1   **Remember two weeks' notice?** Many employers used to give it, but they don't have to—and very few do any more. You can be fired on the spot and find yourself in the parking lot moments later.

2   **They probably don't need good cause to fire you.** Most of us work "at will," which means you can be fired at any time, for any reason that isn't illegal. Even so, you can't be fired for discriminatory reasons, in violation of an employment contract, or for exercising your legal rights. Talk to a lawyer if you suspect foul play.

3   **Get what's coming to you.** You are legally entitled to whatever you've earned and not yet been paid. This includes not only wages but also commissions, bonuses, and, in some states, accrued vacation time.

4   **You might be eligible for unemployment.** To collect unemployment, you must be out of work "through no fault of your own." Many states disqualify only those who were fired for serious misconduct.

5   **Keep your powder dry.** You might be tempted to tell your manager exactly where to get off, but this would be a truly fleeting pleasure. You don't want the company to give you an awful reference (or fight your claim for unemployment).

10   Your Little Legal Companion

**6** **Don't sign anything immediately.** Many companies offer severance (or more severance) only to employees who sign away their right to sue the company. If you're faced with this choice and think you might have a legal claim against your employer, talk to a lawyer right away.

**7** **Everything might be negotiable.** If the company has any concerns about the way it treated you, it might be willing to pay you to go away quietly. Again, a quick consultation with a lawyer will help you figure out if you've got some leverage.

**8** **You'll have to pay to continue your health insurance.** If you had health insurance coverage through your job, you probably have the option to continue receiving it for 18 months or more, through a federal law called COBRA. But you'll have to pay the whole premium.

**9** **Look to the future.** How will you spin this when you're looking for your next job—and who at the company will back up your story? Ask for a letter of reference—and offer to write the first draft yourself.

**10** **The older, wiser you.** An interviewer doesn't want to hear you blame your old boss. Instead, talk about what you learned from the experience and why things will be different in your new position.

Getting Fired 10

## Don't Feel Bad

If you're in the wrong field, getting fired is one of the best things that can happen to you. Plenty of people—from **Thomas Edison** to **Robert Redford** to **Walt Disney**—have been fired, only to go on to great things. Some jobs are just a bad fit.

**Jon Stewart** was fired from his job as a stock clerk at Woolworth's by the assistant manager—his brother. Stewart claims to have been fired by six different stores in the same New Jersey mall.

**Nathaniel Hawthorne** was fired from his position as Surveyor of the Port in the Custom House in Salem, Massachusetts. He used the time (and financial support from his wife and friends) to write *The Scarlet Letter*.

10 Your Little Legal Companion

# Setting Up Shop

## Starting a Business

Whether supplementing your income by selling skateboard parts on the Internet or pursuing a lifelong dream of opening a florist shop, starting a business is one of the great American pastimes. Before you start, there are a few things to consider.

**TEN**
things you
should know

**1  Show yourself the money.** Do the financial plan—how will money come into your business every month, and what will it really cost to operate? Do this on paper, not in your head.

**2  If it's a hobby, it's a hobby . . . and that's okay.** If you don't think you will make a profit, however, you generally cannot deduct the expenses, at least not for long. (The IRS will figure this out, too.)

**3  Use independent contractors when you can.** When you hire employees, it is a whole different ballgame (speaking of pastimes) in terms of responsibilities.

**4  Business is business and friends are friends.** *Never do business with friends*. If you ignore that, don't ignore this: *Never do business with friends without writing down your deal*. That goes for family, too.

**5  Learn from others' mistakes.** If you can, first work (or volunteer) for someone else in the business. Join a trade association. Take someone in the biz to lunch. Everybody remembers their mistakes, and who can resist giving advice?

**6  Use free help.** America's business *is* business, reflected in the myriad of free business resources. Local small business development centers and sba.gov will get you started. For in-person consultations with actual retired businesspeople, go to SCORE (score.org). They've seen it all.

**7**   **Pay attention to your gut (unless you know you are paranoid).** If a deal doesn't seem right, it probably isn't. If it seems too good to be true, it probably is.

**8**   **There are bullies in business, just like in high school.** Never let yourself be rushed into a decision.

**9**   **Be a cheapskate.** Keep your business in your home until your mate wants to leave you. Hold off on hiring an employee until your children threaten to turn you in for violating child labor laws. We exaggerate, but you get the idea.

**10**   **Give yourself a back door.** Commitment and a belief in your business are essential to business success. However, you'll alleviate a lot of anxiety (and get more sleep) if you develop an exit strategy. Cautious optimism is key.

## Humble Beginnings

Forget about renting commercial space for your new venture—the garage will do just fine. You'll be lucky if you fare half as well as these fellows:

- **William Hewlett** and **David Packard** started Hewlett-Packard in a garage in Palo Alto, California.

- **Steve Wozniak** and **Steve Jobs** started Apple Computer in the Jobses' family garage.

- **Gary Clif**, founder of the Clif Bar, was living in a garage with his dog when genius struck.

- **Gary Fisher**, a founder of the sport of mountain biking and owner of Gary Fisher Bikes, began by building bikes in a rented garage in Marin County, California.

- And last but not least … **Jake Warner**, founder of Nolo, wanted to start his business in the garage, but he didn't have one because he was too broke to afford a car. He used the attic instead.

# Growing Your Hard-Earned Cash

**12**

## Investing

Have some extra cash on hand that you don't know what to do with? There are lots of options for investing that money, but you will need to choose carefully to find the best ones for you.

**TEN**
things you
should know

1 **Keep management fees low.** Fees charged to manage mutual funds can wreak havoc on long-term investment performance.

2 **But I want the best.** There is nothing wrong with seeking fund managers with good track records, but keep in mind that on average, only about a quarter of fund managers outperform their relevant index, after fees, in any year; and only one in 10 outperforms for three years running.

3 **Some companies are more equal than others.** The S&P 500 is among the most heavily skewed of the major indexes, with just the top 22 stocks comprising a third of the overall weight or movement of the index. Tying your fortunes to the S&P 500 essentially ties you to the fortunes of a tiny fraction of America's firms.

4 **Are you thinking about the tax benefits?** Some investments have tax advantages, like tax exemptions for municipal bonds and tax deferrals for college or retirement-related obligations.

5 **They know what they're talking about.** Are "fallen stocks" always a good buy? Remember what they say on Wall Street: "Try to catch a falling knife and you'll always get hurt."

**6**  **Like the rest of life, it's all about balance.** Allocating investments across several carefully chosen classes of assets, not all of them stocks and bonds, can help you reduce volatility—without giving up performance.

**7**  **The American way.** Over half of all Americans now own shares of stock, double the figure from the late 1980s.

**8**  **You can put your money where your principles are.** Lots of mutual funds do quite well for investors while steering clear of enterprises that some deem objectionable—whether it's promoting nuclear power, selling cigarettes, or using sweatshop labor.

**9**  **Every year, just like doing taxes.** You will likely get better long-run performance by rebalancing your portfolio annually, which means bringing your investments back to target allocations for the various asset classes.

**10**  **Invest short term and long term.** Choose investments that match your financial timing needs. For short-term investments, consider a money market fund, treasuries, or CDs. Look at stocks, longer maturity bonds, and mutual funds for longer-term investments.

## What about 2106?

A century ago, some of the biggest stocks on the New York Stock Exchange were U.S. Steel, AT&T, Westinghouse, Kodak, Procter and Gamble, Pillsbury, Sears, Kellogg, and Nabisco Crackers.

## Say, what?

The stock market crash of October 19, 1987 is considered one of the most remarkable financial events of the 20th century because the markets fell an astounding 23% worldwide, seemingly without explanation.

# When You Can't Do It Alone

**13**

## Hiring an Employee

Your small business has grown and you need additional help. Congratulations! Before hiring someone, however, consider these points.

**TEN**
things you
should know

1 **Welcome to the thicket.** Hiring an employee immediately subjects you and your business to federal, state, and even county and city laws (and penalties and lawsuits for violating them). So, explore whether independent contractors can meet your needs (but see No. 10).

2 **Putting Junior to work.** If it is your business, you don't owe payroll taxes on wages paid to your child under 18. However, extending family relationships to the workplace can create or exacerbate emotional discord.

3 **Energetic and inexpensive.** It's fine for kids to help around the office, but there are legal limits on the type and amount of work teens can do. Laws for minors doing nonagricultural work are summarized in the Department of Labor's *Child Labor Bulletin 101* (go to dol.gov and search for "childlabor101").

4 **Don't discriminate.** When interviewing, hiring, and managing employees, federal law says you cannot discriminate based on certain characteristics. (Turn the page for that list.) Your state laws or city ordinances may list additional categories.

5 **What does "discriminate" mean, exactly?** It includes basing an employment decision on stereotypes instead of facts and preferring (or excluding) an applicant specifically because of a protected characteristic—for example, not hiring a pregnant woman because you assume she'll quit.

**6** **Checking up.** Besides calling an applicant's references, you may also run a background check. If a third party does the check, you must follow Fair Credit Reporting Act requirements, designed to protect the applicant's privacy. See the Federal Trade Commission's website at www.ftc.gov/os/statutes/fcrajump.htm.

**7** **Employment contract?** You probably don't want one unless you're hiring for a high-level position. Don't accidentally create one, either: Written materials given to new employees (including employee handbooks) should clearly state that they don't create a contract between your business and the employee.

**8** **The record keeping begins.** On the first day, an employee must fill out IRS Form W-4 (for tax purposes) and U.S. Citizenship and Immigration Services Form I-9 (verifying eligibility to work in the United States). You must keep Form I-9s separate from the personnel files and retain them for three years or for one year after an employee's termination, whichever comes first.

**9** **Know thyself.** Understand your own management style before interviewing applicants. Being up-front about how you work and what you expect will help prevent bad feelings during the employment relationship.

**10** **If it were only so.** You can't hire an employee and call him or her an independent contractor. Check IRS Form SS-8 to distinguish the two. Careful here—the federal and state penalties for treating an employee as an independent contractor are severe.

Hiring an Employee 13

*Federal law prohibits discrimination based on:* *

color ● physical or mental disability

religion ● ancestry or national origin

race ● age ● sex ● pregnancy


*Other classes protected by certain cities,*
*counties and states:*


gender identity (transsexualism) ● height or weight

HIV/AIDS ● receipt of public assistance ● marital status

sexual orientation ● smoking


\* All federal antidiscrimination laws make exceptions for very
small businesses, but state and local laws may apply no matter
how few employees you have.

# Down for the Count

14

## When Life Deals You a Physical Blow

We spend our childhoods learning how to take care of ourselves. When involved in an accident or suffering an illness, however, we have to let others take care of us. We've listed a few things to remember when a bad day comes.

**TEN**
things you
should know
• • • • • • • • • • ▶

1 **Embarrassed is better than dead.** Don't be shy about asking (or yelling) for help, even if you feel stupid about tripping over the cat or think that stabbing chest pain is probably just indigestion.

2 **Get thee to the nearest ER.** In a true emergency, when minutes matter, head straight for the nearest hospital, no matter where your insurance plan would normally direct you. Most policies cover emergency visits to hospitals outside the plan network. Even if you're uninsured, federal law requires nearly all hospitals to provide emergency screening examinations and stabilizing treatment.

3 **Allergic to penicillin or latex?** Wear a medic alert necklace or bracelet stating your allergies. Keep a list of current medications in your wallet or purse.

4 **Whose coverage?** If your injury happened on the job, tell your employer, pronto. You'll probably need to be treated under your employer's workers' compensation policy rather than your usual insurance.

5 **Choose hospital advocates.** If you're staying in the hospital, line up your most outspoken friends and family to stay with you. Hospital care varies depending on the quantity and experience of staff, and you may not be able to monitor your own care. Don't worry, you'll be able to return the favor someday.

6   **Who's to blame?** The answer may be "no one" or "my own klutziness." If someone's carelessness caused your injury, however, save physical evidence as best you can, write down the names and contact info of possible witnesses, and take notes about what happened—before you forget the details.

7   **Brush up on that assertiveness training.** Once you are able, don't take no for an answer when it comes to your care. Studies show that patients who monitor their case and loudly express their needs live longer.

8   **Fend off horror stories.** Your injury will inspire others to share their most shocking injury stories. If blood-and-gore tales aren't the tonic you need, prepare a polite but off-putting phrase such as, "I'd love to hear about that sometime when the medication isn't making me so queasy."

9   **Relieve your boredom.** Start keeping a journal or recording your thoughts on tape. If you've broken a bone, ask for a light-colored cast. That way, you can carry around pens and give friends a chance to show their artistic side.

10  **You are not a freak.** Everyone gets injured or sick at some point. In fact, you'll probably start meeting a surprising number of people with the same condition as you.

## *Weird Medical Fact*

Sofas or couches injured over 135,000 people in 2002 badly enough to seek medical attention! Skateboards sent only 113,000 people to the doctor.

# Show Me the Credit Card Debt

**15**

## Borrowing Money

In the mail, on TV, online, everywhere you go someone is offering you "free" cash. Before you take that loan, here are ten things you should know about borrowing money.

1 **But Ben Franklin said to pay it off early!** Some bank or credit card loans come with a prepayment penalty. In states where these penalties are permitted, it's usually not worth paying off the loan early.

2 **Keep it in the family.** If you're borrowing from friends or family, consider using CircleLending (www.circlelending.com), which doesn't lend money but facilitates loans by helping prepare the loan agreement and managing the payment process.

3 **Don't count on bankruptcy.** The new bankruptcy law makes it more difficult to wipe out some debts, and you can only file bankruptcy once every six to eight years, depending on the kind of bankruptcy you file.

4 **But for the grace of ….** When taking a cash advance from a credit card company, there is usually no grace period—which means you pay interest from the day you take the cash, *even* if you pay off your balance within a month.

5 **Watch your ratings.** The most important factor in your credit rating: paying debts on time. Other factors: type of credit, amount owed, length of credit history, and how much debt you have relative to your available credit.

6 **It's not so secret.** The Fair Credit Reporting Act requires each of the consumer reporting companies to provide, at your request, a free copy of your credit report, once every 12 months.

**7** **The 80% rule.** Experts say that you shouldn't charge business expenses if your credit card balances are greater than 80% of your credit limits. If you're in that situation, you've already got a serious credit card problem.

**8** **Predators at your door.** The most common predatory lending practice is placing a borrower into a higher interest rate than the credit risk calls for. An estimated 63% of borrowers paying high rates would qualify for lower ones.

**9** **Your corporate shield won't help.** If you've incorporated your business but personally guarantee a business loan, your personal assets are not protected from creditors. The buck doesn't stop at your business; it can stop at your home or personal bank account.

**10** **Leave me alone!** If you want to stop getting all those preapproved credit card offers (and save who knows how many trees), call the Federal Trade Commission's "opt-out" number, 888-567-8688, and you'll get a five-year reprieve.

# Fun Facts About Borrowing in the U.S.

- The U.S. has 300 million people and over a billion credit cards.

- Personal debt (not counting mortgages) is approximately $20,000 per household, half of which is on credit cards. (That's three times what it was in 1990.)

- Over 40% of families routinely spend more each year than they earn.

- The average U.S. family pays about $1,200 in interest on their cards each year, at an average APR of 18.9%.

- In 2004, the total spent on credit card fees topped $60 billion.

- Fifty percent of Americans would refuse to tell a friend how much they owe.

# May It Never Happen to You or Yours

**16**

## Trouble With the Law

Lawyers take criminal law classes in law school, but until they're trying cases, it's all theory. Here's the low-down from the street, the holding cell, and the courtroom.

**TEN**
things you
should know

• • • • • • • • • • ▶

1 **Federal crimes have stiffer sentences than state offenses.** Knocking off a bank is a federal offense and usually carries more time than a convenience store robbery.

2 **What suspects blurt out can and will be used against them.** The Miranda rule protects defendants only if they're being questioned.

3 **If the door is open, savvy suspects use it.** Speaking of Miranda, the cops must read these rights before questioning only when their target is in custody. When suspects are free to leave but answer anyway, their "un-Mirandized" statements can be used against them.

4 **The cops can violate Miranda but still use a suspect's statements if he testifies.** One more thing about that famous case: If defendants testify and have made un-Mirandized statements that contradict their testimony, the prosecutor can use them to discredit that testimony.

5 **Thanks, but could I have a real lawyer?** Many defendants get their families to pay big money to hire private counsel instead of going with the public defender. Private counsel may not know how to broker the best deal. Defendants are usually better off with a home-court player.

**6  Seasoned criminals won't tell their lawyers they're going to lie on the stand.** The lawyer will withdraw from the case, without saying why. But everyone will figure it out, and any chance of sympathy from the judge (at sentencing) will go out the window.

**7  Cops and prosecutors follow the money.** Burglars and robbers will be tempted to change their spending habits—why else did they get all that cash? Sudden lavish vacations and toys have only one reasonable explanation, which juries understand.

**8  The Shawshank Redemption is fiction.** Prison inmates have names like Dagger and Skullcrusher—the names of male inmates are even scarier.

**9  Appealing a conviction is an exercise in futility.** The overwhelming majority are denied. Defendants can't reopen their cases—they're limited to arguing that the judge made legal errors. Judges decide appeals. You get the picture.

**10  Only the foolish represent themselves.** Yes, you heard it from Nolo, the champion of do-it-yourself law. There's no way a defendant can match the resources and wiliness of the cops and prosecutors. Anyone with any sense will hire an attorney who specializes in criminal defense, whose office is not across the street from the courthouse or next to the bail bondsman.

Trouble With the Law  16

## *Stupid Criminal Tricks*

Defendants aren't supposed to identify the victim in the lineup. Yes, it's true. Some participants in lineups think they're supposed to ID the victim. It's the other way around.

# Just Call Me Shawna

**17**

## Changing Your Name

Whether you are getting married or divorced,
are changing sexes, or simply feel "Dorcas"
or "Wilbur" never expressed the real you,
changing your moniker is relatively easy.

**1** **You don't need a good reason, just a legal one.** You can change your name for any purpose short of breaking the law—and you can do it without a lawyer.

**2** **Getting hitched?** You don't need a court order to change your name, just your marriage certificate.

**3** **If you're simply tired of your old name, go to court and get a new one.** You'll have to fill out some court papers, but they're fairly simple. The hard part is deciding what you want to be called—will it be Sunflower? Just Jack?

**4** **Filing court papers won't be scary.** You'll probably never even have to appear before a judge.

**5** **You can choose (almost) any name you want.** There are only a few restrictions: Don't change your name for a fraudulent purpose. Don't take a famous person's name. Stay away from names that are overtly offensive. Copyrighted or trademarked names are also off limits—so sorry, you can't be Harry Potter. Finally, it's best to avoid numerals and punctuation—in other words, don't call yourself "?" or "3."

**6** **You can change your name to a single word.** If you've always wanted to be like Madonna, now's your chance. You can't take her name, but you can choose one word, or even just initials, as your name.

7   **You might have to pay a few hundred dollars for the new you.** Unless you qualify to change your name as part of another legal proceeding, such as a divorce, the fees may run as high as $500. (Twice as much if you hire a lawyer to do the job.)

8   **One-stop shopping.** If you're changing genders, some states allow you to change the sex on your birth certificate at the same time you change your name.

9   **The one easy thing to get in a divorce is your former name.** In most states you can simply ask the judge to make a formal order restoring your name as part of the divorce decree.

10  **Don't keep it a secret.** Besides advising agencies and businesses that you've changed your name, you'll want to encourage your family and friends to use only your new name— and be sure to use it consistently yourself to avoid practical, administrative, and personal hassles.

*Do you think* the name made all the difference? These famous people started life with the monikers in parentheses after their names:

- Alan Alda (Alphonso D'Abruzzo)
- Woody Allen (Allen Konigsberg)
- Lauren Bacall (Betty Joan Perske)
- Jon Bon Jovi (John Francis Bongiovi)
- Bono (Paul David Hewson)
- George Burns (Nathan Birnbaum)
- Chubby Checker (Ernest Evans)
- Elvis Costello (Declan Patrick McManus)
- 50 Cent (Curtis Jackson)
- Whoopi Goldberg (Caryn Johnson)
- Hulk Hogan (Terry Gene Bollea)
- Ben Kingsley (Krishna Bhanji)
- Ralph Lauren (Ralph Lifshitz)
- Ludacris (Chris Bridges)
- Marilyn Manson (Brian Warner)
- Meat Loaf (Marvin Lee Aday)
- Demi Moore (Demetria Gene Guynes)
- Mother Teresa (Agnes Gonxha Bojaxhiu)

# Finding the Right Spot

**18**

## When You Start the House Search

Thinking about acquiring your first home or condo? You may feel like you're searching for a needle in a haystack, particularly if the housing market is tight where you plan to live. Here's how veteran house hunters make the right choice without becoming overwhelmed.

**TEN**
things you
should know

1 **Be patient.** Your real estate guardian angel may not help you buy the first house you fall in love with—but there will always be more houses for sale. Hey, you were heartbroken over your ninth-grade breakup, but aren't you glad now?

2 **Guzzle some gas (er, get out your bikes).** You're probably not as well acquainted with your favorite—or second-choice—neighborhood as you think. By methodically following every street in an area, you may find a great one you never knew existed.

3 **Look past the staging.** Sellers are getting expert at turning a ho-hum house into a seeming B&B-to-be. Try to picture the bare shell that'll be left after all the flowers, antique furniture, and adorable knickknacks are gone.

4 **Tell everyone you know that you're house hunting.** Friends of friends may be planning to sell their house and would like to save some effort (and commissions) by selling directly to you.

5 **Scrape together the biggest down payment you can manage.** The higher your down payment, the more house you can afford. If this means holding a garage sale, packing sandwiches to work, or collecting the money your feckless brother borrowed from you last year, go for it.

**6** **Ask around for a great real estate agent.** However, don't expect the agent to do all the work. No one truly understands what you're seeking better than you, so scan the classifieds and check online for interesting houses.

**7** **You're allowed to touch.** Open windows, try water faucets, and check closets. You may discover problems or get an idea of how well the house has been maintained.

**8** **How much is a house worth?** Whatever someone is willing to pay. To determine a reasonable price, visit open houses and ask your realtor for "comps," that is, what houses with similar characteristics in the same neighborhood have sold for. You'll then be ready to make an educated bid on the house you want.

**9** **Review the seller's inspection reports with a jaundiced eye.** Sellers may not be quite as interested as you in finding all the flaws in their properties. Hire an obsessively careful inspector, and make your purchase offer contingent on satisfaction with the findings.

**10** **You can change your mind about home ownership.** In most parts of the country, the same monthly payment will rent you a better house in a nicer neighborhood than where you could afford to buy. And better yet, you can call the landlord when the roof starts to leak.

## *Got ghosts?*

If your house is haunted by unfriendly spirits, here are some reportedly effective ways to be rid of them. Just don't forget to take a picture of your unwanted visitors first.

- Ask the ghosts to leave (maybe this should have been obvious, but a firm voice apparently helps).

- Hang strings of hazelnuts in all doorways.

- Sprinkle holy water (available at your local Catholic church) while making the sign of the cross.

- Hang cloves of garlic from all doors and windows.

- Ring a bell in every corner of every room.

- Paint your front door red.

# Welcome to the Neighborhood

**19**

## Being a Good Neighbor

Home should be your sanctuary from a stressful world. Creating good relationships with your neighbors will help keep it that way.

**TEN**
things you
should know

• • • • • • • • • • ▶

1 **Don't be shy.** Take the first step and introduce yourself to your neighbors. If it feels comfortable, you may want to exchange phone numbers and other basic information, like how many children and pets you each have. It may help in an emergency or when, as you drive to the airport, you realize you left the garage door open.

2 **Join in.** Learn about neighborhood concerns at neighborhood or tenants' associations meetings. Whether it's broken street lamps, a new commercial development, or a burglar, you'll be better able to protect yourself (and maybe make some new friends, too).

3 **Probably the most common neighbor complaint?** Excessive noise, whether a loud TV or early-morning leaf blowing. Your town or state probably has a noise ordinance—follow it. If you're hosting a big party, let your immediate neighbors know ahead of time. Better yet, include them.

4 **You and Mother Nature.** Trees on your property are your responsibility. Keep limbs trimmed to avoid being sued if one falls on your neighbor's car. Trees on a property line are the joint responsibility of the property owners.

5 **What do you mean, my curtains have to be white?** Find out whether you can live with community homeowner rules (called Conditions, Covenants, & Restrictions or CC&Rs) *before* you move into a condominium or other planned neighborhood.

6  **"Adverse possession"?** Sounds ugly, and it is. Under this legal doctrine, a person can gain rights to part of your property by using it *without* your permission for several years. You can prevent this by giving written permission to neighbors who want to use your property as a shortcut or as part of their driveway. Describe the property in question in detail and include a sentence reserving your right to withdraw the permission in the future.

7  **It takes a village.** Property owners must make safe any conditions on their land that might injure children—for example, swimming pools, unsafe structures, even natural conditions. Look over your property from a child's point of view.

8  **Good fences make good neighbors?** Some people think so. Before building a new fence, review local laws that restrict fence height and placement.

9  **Yes, he's cute, but.** If you have a dog, follow your local leash and noise laws. Fence your yard to keep Scruffy from using your neighbors' property as his playground (or toilet).

10  **Record your agreement.** Any agreements you make with your neighbors (for instance, permission to use part of your land, or agreement about who owns a boundary fence) should be written down, signed by everyone concerned, and filed in the county recorder's office where the property is located.

Being a Good Neighbor  19

## Bless This House

One traditional house blessing for a new neighbor involves salt, milk and honey, and oil—and banging on pots and pans. First, sprinkle salt at each door and window (don't forget the dog door); this symbolizes purification. Next, sprinkle milk and honey at each door and window; this symbolizes prosperity and peace. Third, anoint each door and window with a bit of oil; this symbolizes sealing the house to keep the good in and the bad out. Finally—and this is fun at a housewarming party—bang on pots and pans at every door and window to shoo out any bad energy. (Just don't do this in the middle of the night unless you want the police to show up.)

# But When Will My Jessica Play?

20

## When You Elect to Be a Coach

It may be your turn to coach your son's soccer team, or you may have had to compete for the position. However you end up in the job, keep a few things in mind.

**TEN**
things you
should know

1 **When they're only three feet tall.** Make sure your overall coaching style and program are appropriate for your group. Is it pee wee soccer, a division 1 high school baseball team, or a masters' swim team? If you lean toward a Bobby Knight personality, stay away from the little tykes (or start taking some medication).

2 **But I never played lacrosse.** You don't have to be proficient, but you need to get up to speed on any special skills, drills, or coaching methods used in your sport. Go online, ask the high school athletic department for tips, or watch other teams practice.

3 **Winning?** Sorry, Vince, it really isn't everything. You want athletes to gain self-confidence, learn skills, and have fun. Create a positive experience for them by rewarding effort and success. Then go reward yourself for your own patience and effort.

4 **Have a game plan for each season and each practice.** Have a big-picture goal and create a plan to reach that goal. For each practice, go prepared with plenty of drills, exercises, and activities to keep your athletes busy and motivated.

5 **Communication is key.** Learn to talk (and listen) to your athletes as a team and individually. If you're coaching kids, you will also have to communicate and deal with parents—good luck.

**6  Why is he always the goalie?** Nothing undermines your relationship with individuals or the group more quickly than being unfair. Fair treatment earns your athletes' and opponents' trust and respect.

**7  Safety first.** Have a cell phone and basic first aid kit at all practices and games. CPR training is a plus. Are there any health or safety requirements particular to your sport? Have all medical releases been submitted by athletes? With adults, requiring a physical exam may be appropriate.

**8  Keep your eyes open.** Watch for problems related to nutrition, drugs, overtraining, and abuse. Talk to your league members, school administrators, or athletic associations about what to do if you see troubling signs.

**9  Check for proper insurance coverage.** If your group has a governing body or association, insurance is often included as part of the group affiliation fee.

**10  Behave.** Know and follow the rules of conduct and ethics that govern your sport. Try not to use professional teams as your guide.

When You Elect to Be a Coach  20

## Think Positive

The Positive Coaching Alliance was created to help coaches teach kids not only to win but also to love sports and learn lifelong skills. It holds workshops for coaches and parents, and partners with youth sports organizations and schools. Check it out at www.positivecoach.org.

> *"I've learned that people will forget what you said, people will forget what you did, but people will never forget how you made them feel."*
>
> **—Maya Angelou**

# What's My Name Again?

21

## When Your Identity Is Stolen

You've just been turned down for a home equity loan. You got a call from an obnoxious bill collector about an account you don't recognize. You've noticed you're no longer receiving the usual five credit card offers per day. If your credit is generally good, you may have had your identity stolen. If you are experiencing serious harassment or been arrested based on someone else's criminal activities, getting a lawyer makes sense. Otherwise, you probably can handle the mess yourself. Here are some things to get you started.

**TEN**
things you
should know

• • • • • • • • • ▶

1 **Time, patience, and a feeling of security.** You'll lose all of them when your identity is stolen. In most cases, however, you won't lose much money if you respond quickly and tenaciously.

2 **Call each credit agency.*** Report you've been a victim of identity theft. Request a free copy of your credit report, to which you're entitled in fraud situations. Ask that a fraud alert and victim's statement be placed in your file, helping prevent additional loss—but also hindering your legitimate efforts to obtain credit.

3 **Create a log.** Use a spiral-bound notebook so little pieces of paper don't disappear. For every call or other task, record the details, the time spent, to whom you spoke, and their contact information.

4 **File a police report.** You'll need a police report or case number and contact information for credit agencies and creditors. Don't expect justice, however.

5 **Inspect your credit reports.** Note everything that looks wrong (including former job listings and addresses—the thief probably listed some), and send a letter listing errors to each agency. They are required to correct and send you a new, free report. Repeat if necessary.

6 **Contact each account's fraud department.** Close the questionable account (ask that closure be noted as "at customer's request"). Frustration alert: To speak to customer service, you're

required to enter the relevant account number, which you probably don't have because somebody else opened the account. If stymied, call a different department and ask to be transferred. Then always get the direct number and your contact's name.

7 **Make friends with a notary public.** You'll have to file an affidavit (a sworn written statement) with every credit account involved. Some will accept the form on the Federal Trade Commission (FTC) website; others will want something different. Regardless, it'll probably have to be notarized (look in the yellow pages), for which you will pay a fee.

8 **Copy everything you mail.** Send it certified, return receipt requested. Keep copies in a folder.

9 **There's more?!** Enter your case information in the FTC identity fraud database. Contact every agency appropriate to your circumstances. If someone is using your Social Security number, alert the Social Security Administration. If you think your driver's license or passport was used or stolen, contact your local department of motor vehicles or the U.S. State Department, respectively. If someone opened a post office box in your name, contact the postal service.

10 **On the bright side.** Losses from theft are tax-deductible. If you itemize, include all your costs (including your time).

\* Contact information for the agencies mentioned here is listed on the next page.

When Your Identity Is Stolen 21

## Numbers You'll Need

- Credit agencies:
  - Equifax: 800-525-6285 or www.equifax.com
  - Experian: 888-397-3742 or www.experian.com
  - TransUnion: 800-680-7289 or www.transunion.com

- Federal Trade Commission
  www.consumer.gov/idtheft

- Identity Theft Hotline at 877-438-4338

- Social Security Administration
  www.socialsecurity.gov/oig/guidelin.htm

- SSA Fraud Hotline at 800-269-0271

- U.S. State Department
  www.travel.state.gov/passport/index.html
  202-955-0430

- U.S. Postal Service (to locate your local postal inspector)
  www.usps.com/ncsc/locators/find-is.html
  800-275-8777

# The Incredible Unpleasantness of Being a Litigant

## 22

## Getting Sued

There's nothing worse than that sinking feeling you get when you are handed a legal document that announces you're being sued. Say hello to lawyers, courtrooms, big bills, sour stomachs, and sleepless nights. Here are things you may not know about being on the receiving end of a lawsuit.

1 **You're it.** You don't have to "accept" the papers that begin the lawsuit. You just have to be "given" the papers … which can mean that the server announced what the papers were and then presented them to you … even if you throw them on the ground. (p.s. That may earn you a citation for littering!)

2 **No service advantage.** The plaintiffs—the persons filing the suit--lose their cases about half the time they go to trial in state courts.

3 **The purse is shrinking.** Even when plaintiffs win, their financial awards are smaller. The median award in state court jury trials fell to $37,000 during the 1990s—less than half of what it had been before 1992.

4 **It's all about the pregame.** Fewer than 3% of the civil lawsuits filed go to trial, so it's unlikely you'll end up being grilled in the witness box.

5 **Watch what you sign.** You have a right to a jury trial in a civil dispute unless you signed away that right by agreeing to arbitration.

6 **Five top reasons civil lawsuits are filed:** contract disputes, personal injuries, disputes over property, disputes over estates, and family disputes such as custody and divorce proceedings.

**7**  **Just the facts, ma'am.** Witnesses (except for expert and character witnesses) can generally testify only about things they observed, not what they heard.

**8**  **The emotional hook.** Lawyers love clients who sue over "principle," because their cases usually go on longer than those brought solely for economic reasons. If you're a defendant, resist the urge to countersue unless you have a solid case. See a therapist instead—they're cheaper than lawyers, and you'll feel a whole lot better.

**9**  **Forget Perry Mason.** A jury doesn't always consist of 12 people. Instead, in many states or federal courts, your case may be decided by nine or even six people.

**10**  **Address the stress.** As a defendant, you will likely be insulted, enraged, and incredulous. Take some time to blow off some steam. More golf or more yoga, whatever will help.

Getting sued  22

## How frivolous is frivolous?

Let's see ... there was the little league coach in Ohio who, after a 0-15 season, was sued for bad coaching. Then, there was the man who sued the bank he robbed after being burned by tear gas from an exploding security pack. Then there was the woman who claimed injuries after sitting next to an obese woman on an airplane. Then there was the lady who sued the makers of a snack food for incorrectly listing the calorie count. And of course there was the writer who was sued for defaming a convicted serial killer.

# Anything but Simple

## Becoming a Landlord

Whether you hope to become a land baron
or simply to raise a little extra cash by renting
out the in-law apartment in your basement,
renting property is a lot trickier than it looks. If
you decide to do it, take some precautions.

**TEN**
things you
should know

• • • • • • • • • ➤

1 **Do the legwork.** Always check applicants' credit history, references, and background, even if you "have a good feeling" about them. Haphazard screening often results in problem tenants who don't pay rent, trash your place, move in undesirable friends, or worse. Another bad result? Lower property value.

2 **Put it on paper.** The best way to avoid tenant lawsuits and complaints is to document everything: the rental application and lease, when and how you handle repair requests, and the notice you give to enter a tenant's apartment or end the tenancy.

3 **"That's my money!"** Tenants will go to the mat over their security deposit. To avoid disputes, follow state law when setting, collecting, holding, and returning deposits. Inspect and photograph the property at move-in and move-out times, and document all deductions for repair and damage.

4 **A leaky toilet can cost you its weight in gold.** Failure to maintain your property and handle complaints quickly can lead to tenants withholding rent, suing you for injuries, or moving out without notice.

5 **Crime means you pay.** You can be liable for thousands of dollars in tenant losses if your rental property is an easy mark. Landlords are sued more than any other business owners, with the average settlement paid by a landlord's insurance company (in safety cases) equaling over half a million dollars.

**6**    **Your tenants' home is their castle.** Give at least 24 hours' notice (or the minimum required by your state law) before entering a rental unit, and make sure it's for a good reason, such as making repairs. FYI, snooping to determine whether your tenant is a "boxer or brief man" is not a good reason.

**7**    **What you can't see can hurt you.** Landlords are liable for tenant health problems from exposure to a rental property's environmental hazards, which may include mold. Most states also require you to disclose lead-based paint hazards.

**8**    **Say hello to your alter ego.** If you hire a property manager who illegally discriminates against tenants, fails to comply with landlord-tenant laws, or is simply incompetent, you're the one who could be held financially responsible. Supervise your manager carefully.

**9**    **Don't even think about skimping on insurance.** Good liability and property insurance are absolute must-haves to protect your property from fire, storms, burglary, vandalism, personal injury, and lawsuits.

**10**    **Call your tenant before you call your lawyer, even if you dread it.** Unless you need to immediately evict a tenant, for example, over unpaid rent or drug dealing, try to resolve the problem informally, through mediation by a neutral third party, or in small claims court. Nothing raises emotional stakes and costs like the letters a-t-t-o-r-n-e-y.

## *Want to play The Landlord's Game?*

Monopoly is the best-selling board game in the world, with over 200 million games sold (in 26 different languages, including Croatian). According to the official Monopoly website (www.hasbro.com/monopoly), the game was invented by an unemployed inventor, Charles B. Darrow of Germantown, Pennsylvania, in the mid-1930s. Some claim that the real inspiration for Monopoly was Lizzie Magie, a Quaker from Virginia who received a patent for The Landlord's Game in 1904, in which all the properties are rented (not acquired as in Monopoly). Parker Brothers reportedly bought The Landlord's Game for $500 with no royalties and marketed a few hundred copies before stopping distribution. See www.antimonopoly.com for details.

# How Hard Could It Be?

24

## Your First "Do-It-Yourself" Home Improvement Project

You have just bought a house and your cash reserves are tapped out. Work needs to be done, and you're excited about doing it yourself. If you haven't done this before, read over our list before embarking on a home project.

TEN
things you
should know

• • • • • • • • • •▶

1 **DIY doesn't mean free.** You may be shocked at the cost of materials, especially lumber. Explore alternative materials before you buy. Also, consider what you cost. Working on your property as a hobby is one thing; it's another if you're taking time away from a lucrative business. What do you normally earn per hour? How does that compare to an experienced contractor?

2 **How much will you use that reciprocating saw?** Few things are more fun than buying new tools for a project, but calculate how much you're willing to invest before you're in the store. If your project requires new tools you'll never use again, rent (or hire the pro).

3 **Make friends.** Find a good hardware store, with employees who actually know the products and how to use them. The best stores employ retired tradespeople (plumbers, electricians, painters). Many are happy to walk you through your project, and their tips about common mistakes can save you a lot of frustration.

4 **Remember the number 3.** No project of any complexity involves fewer than three trips to the hardware store. And every project will take at least three times as long as you think it will.

5 **Sunday night heartbreak.** Never start a home improvement project on a Sunday morning--most hardware stores close early. Begin first thing on Saturday and make sure no one is coming for dinner.

6  **Don't drink too much coffee.** If you have to turn off the water at the main valve for your project, will you be able to complete it and turn the water on again soon? Remember, no one can flush.

7  **Respect electricity.** There are many dangers to avoid in home improvement, but especially so with electrical projects. You really must know what you're doing. The steps are simple, the mistakes are grave.

8  **Some of our favorite phrases.** "Measure twice, cut once." (You know what that means.) "Righty-tighty, lefty-loosy." To tighten a bolt, turn it right. To loosen it, turn it left. "We can make it work." When you're really good, you can say it.

9  **Unfinished business.** Perhaps the most difficult part of a DIY project is the last step. Reward yourself if you can finish the project before listing the house to sell—otherwise you'll be staring at that missing piece of trim for five years.

10  **If you finished, congratulations!** If you didn't, there's no shame in defeat. Just call a pro—they're used to it. But wait! Be sure you call for the right reinforcements. Get recommendations from trusted sources—perhaps the very people who advised you at the hardware store.

Your First "Do-It-Yourself" Home Improvement Project    24

## If Your House Is Ready for Its Close-up

Are you in desperate need of a home renovation
—and do you have a compelling story? If so, consider,
applying to the popular TV show *Extreme Makeover: Home
Edition*. If your house is in really bad shape—and your
family's situation is heartbreaking—a team of designers,
contractors, and workers will rebuild and decorate your
entire house (inside and out) in just seven days. You'll
need to make a short video on why your family needs a
home makeover and complete a lengthy application
(be prepared to report any lawsuits you've been involved
in or criminal convictions). For details, see http://abc
.go.com/primetime/xtremehome/casting.html.

# The New Market

## Buying and Selling on eBay

Back in 1995, Pierre Omidyar had a website
and a broken laser pointer. So he posted his
laser pen on his website and allowed bidding.
He was shocked when it sold for $14.83.
Several billion dollars later, Omidyar and
cofounder Jeff Skoll have created a trend, an
industry, and a marketing phenomenon. If
you're new to eBay, here are ten tips to get
you started in this online marketplace.

**TEN**
things you
should know

1 **Say it right in under 50 characters.** Your auction title is key to customer searches and sales. Use a title that conforms to what similar sellers are using, and watch your spelling.

2 **Curious as to how many people are viewing your auctions?** Use one of the free visit counters that measure your hits and can even compare the number to hits for similar auctions in the same category.

3 **Use software tools.** If you want to become a high-volume seller (or buyer), there are plenty of software tools available to help, including market research software, listing software, and bidding software. Type "ebay tools" into your Internet search engine.

4 **eBay's top ten.** Wondering what the most popular eBay categories are? Here they are, in order of popularity: Collectibles, Clothing, Shoes & Accessories, Entertainment, Sports, Home, Jewelry & Watches, Computers & Electronics, Toys & Hobbies, Books, and Pottery & Glass.

5 **Pay attention to auction end times.** While one study showed that only 15% of auctions are decided in the final 60 seconds, don't end your auction in the middle of the night. And if you want to participate in the sniping (the term for bidding in the final seconds), use a software tool (search for "snipe software" on the Internet).

**6**   **Prevent phishing.** If you're concerned about fraudulent (spoof) eBay or PayPal websites, download the eBay toolbar. It comes with a feature called Account Guard, which warns users when they reach a spoof website.

**7**   **R U NARU?** eBay users have a host of acronyms at their disposal (for example, NM means "near mint"; BIN refers to a Buy It Now sale). If you're unsure of the meaning, check out the Acronyms page in eBay's Help section.

**8**   **No reservations.** Most eBay experts advise against using a reserve price (the unlisted amount below which you don't have to sell) for your listings. Reserves reportedly turn off many bidders.

**9**   **Haben Sie eBay?** eBay now permits you to list items on eBay Germany and eBay UK, and soon expects to permit listings on other international eBay sites as well.

**10**   **It's all about the feedback.** The genius of eBay is that it was created as a community, and members' feedback is important. Build up positive feedback from your buyers and sellers, and provide good communication and service so you don't get negative comments.

Buying and Selling on eBay   25

## *Some of the Oddities Offered on eBay*

- belly-button lint

- horse hoof ashtray

- combination bicycle/lawn mower

- toenail clippings

- Britney spears gum (ABC or "already been chewed")

- human kidney (eBay pulled the auction before the sale completed)

- the right to permanently tattoo an advertisement on a woman's forehead (sold for $10,000)

- contents of a trashcan

- piece of Nutri-Grain resembling ET

- several tablespoons of water, reportedly from a cup Elvis Presley once drank from

# Author! Author!

## 26

### Writing a Book

Someone once said there are three difficulties for a writer: writing something worth publishing, finding an honest company to publish it, and getting people to read it. Gee, is that all? We've listed some things that every fledgling author should know.

1   **What's the secret of hitting the bestseller lists?** Don't ask
    your publisher. Michael Korda of Simon & Schuster wrote a history
    of bestsellers and reported: "Publishers find it so hard to repeat
    their success [because] half the time they can't figure out how
    they happened in the first place." Only half?

2   **Wondering why books sales have gone flat?** Blame the
    Internet. The average American spends more time on the Internet
    (about three hours a week) than reading books (two hours a week).

3   **Don't worry too much about copyright.** If you created
    the book by yourself, you get copyright automatically. However,
    registering it with the U.S. Copyright Office (www.copyright.gov)
    can enhance your rights.

4   **It takes two to tangle.** If you're writing with a coauthor, make
    sure you sort out the rights and obligations of each coauthor
    before you begin work. The easiest way to do it is with a coauthor
    agreement.

5   **Vanity publishing (when you pay a publisher to print
    your book) is rarely worth the money.** If you're not getting
    the editing, marketing, and distribution offered by a regular
    publisher, you're better off simply printing your own copies.
    Figure out the costs online by typing "printing cost estimator" into
    your search engine.

**6**  **Numbers can be deceiving.** Don't get too excited when your Amazon.com sales number jumps one or two thousand digits in a day. That may only reflect sales of one or two books ... and those sales are only at Amazon.

**7**  **Sales may be flat, but new books keep on coming.** Never have so many books competed for shelf space in the U.S.—over 1,000 new titles a week, twice the volume of a decade ago.

**8**  **What's the scariest (and least read) provision in your book contract?** It could be the indemnity provision, which commonly requires an author to pay the publisher's legal costs if anybody sues over the book's contents.

**9**  **Looking for an agent?** Be wary of those who charge for a reading fee, or who charge more than 20% commission on domestic sales or more than 25% for overseas sales.

**10**  **Don't quit your job yet.** The average nonfiction trade book sells 2,000 copies in its first year. Average numbers for novels are even lower. On the other hand, every year there are bestsellers, too. If you want to write, sit down and write! Just don't call your novel a memoir.

Writing a Book  26

## And They Should Know

*Writing a novel is a terrible experience, during which the hair often falls out and the teeth decay.*

**—Flannery O'Connor**

*Writing is more than anything a compulsion, like some people wash their hands thirty times a day for fear of awful consequences.*

**—Julie Burchill**

*Writing is not a profession, but a vocation of unhappiness.*

**—Georges Simenon**

*The writer has a grudge against society, which he documents with accounts of unsatisfying sex, unrealized ambition, unmitigated loneliness, and a sense of distress.*

**—Renata Adler**

*Writing is really horribly hard and I mistrust writers who say it's fun. Writing is a lot of fun—after you've done it. Beginning it is painful and you always think you've forgotten how.*

**—Roger Angell**

 Your Little Legal Companion

# Freedom's Just Another Word for Nothing Left to Lose

## Surviving Bankruptcy

Everybody runs into trouble at one time or another. If you are up against the wall financially, you'll want to know some information about the bankruptcy option.

**TEN**
things you
should know

1. **The new bankruptcy law isn't as bad as you might have heard.** Most people can still file for Chapter 7, keep all of their property, and have much of their debt wiped out.

2. **Don't feel guilty.** Bankruptcy exists because the legal system recognizes that debts can get the better of even the most conscientious among us. Bankruptcy is your chance for a fresh start. Take advantage of it, if you need to.

3. **Think through your options.** The best solution to your debt problems—liquidating your debt through Chapter 7 bankruptcy, repaying some of it through Chapter 13 bankruptcy, or taking steps outside the bankruptcy system—depends on your personal situation, including what you earn, what you own, and what you owe.

4. **Keep your phone number.** Laws protect you from being hounded by creditors, even if you don't file for bankruptcy.

5. **Sharpen your pencil.** When you file for bankruptcy, you will have to complete lots of paperwork. It's important to be thorough and accurate—if you aren't, your case could be thrown out.

6. **Don't file an emergency petition.** Although you have the option of filing some of your paperwork right away and the rest later, most people who go this route end up in trouble because they blow the deadline for turning in the rest of their forms.

 Your Little Legal Companion

**7**  **Think twice before reaffirming credit card debts.** Most credit card debt is erased in bankruptcy, so it rarely makes sense to reaffirm (agree to continue owing) that debt, no matter what the credit card company tells you.

**8**  **Avoid additional temptation.** Believe it or not, going bankrupt will not stop the endless stream of credit card offers in your mailbox—but you'll find that they come with much higher interest rates.

**9**  **Make a budget.** Yes, it's boring, but tracking your expenses and creating a budget is the best way to figure out how to live within your means. Try carrying around a notebook for a month to record all of your expenses.

**10**  **Know your rights.** Some creditors will keep trying to collect a debt—by calling, garnishing your wages, or even suing you—after it was wiped out in bankruptcy. This is illegal, and you can put a stop to it.

## *Is that why they call it Chapter 7?*

*"At the end of every seven years thou shalt make a release.*

*And this is the manner of the release: Every creditor that lendeth ought unto his neighbour shall release it; he shall not exact it of his neighbour, or of his brother."*

**—Deuteronomy 15:1-2 (King James Bible)**

# Who Ate the Last Piece of Pie?

28

## Moving in With Your Lover

Making the commitment to move in together is a big step in any relationship, and adjustments of all sorts are necessary. Before you merge your books and CDs, take some time to understand some of the legal aspects of your step.

**TEN**
things you
should know

1 **Those wild seniors.** Cohabitation is especially popular among the over-60 set. Marriage can negatively affect Social Security benefits, so many seniors opt to live together instead.

2 **Unless it's in writing, you don't have the same rights as marrieds.** Unmarried couples who live together don't inherit from each other without a will that says so, and without a power of attorney neither has the right to make medical decisions for the other if he or she is unable to make them.

3 **Unmarried couples also don't have the same responsibilities.** In the event of a breakup, it is unlikely one partner, even the primary earner, will be required to pay alimony to the other. However, a court may enforce one partner's specific promise to support the other.

4 **Domestic what?** A common term for unmarried couples who live together, "domestic partnership" now has a specific legal meaning in a number of states. In most of these states, you can register as domestic partners only if you are a same-sex couple or one of you is over 62.

5 **Avoid unnecessary heartache.** Write down how you will or won't share money and property. What happens when one of you buys a piece of furniture or when you buy a big-ticket item together? No fancy agreement is necessary, as long as it's clear and you both sign it.

**6** **That goes double for buying houses together.** If you want to own a house together, put both your names on the deed. Record your agreement about how you'll pay for repairs and improvements, and what happens to the house if you break up.

**7** **What about kids?** Unmarried opposite-sex partners who have children are the legal parents of the children. In a breakup, both are responsible for supporting the children, and both have custody rights.

**8** **Love and a tax benefit, too.** You may be able to claim your live-in partner as a dependent on your tax return if you provide more than half of his or her support and he or she earns $2,900 or less per year.

**9** **More good news.** Unless you are registered domestic partners, you are not automatically responsible for your partner's debts. If you borrow money together, however, you are each responsible for the entire loan, and a creditor can come after you for the whole amount if your partner flakes out.

**10** **That was the easy stuff.** Now it's up to you to decide how to deal with a paucity of closet space and your partner's propensity to leave dishes in the sink.

*Come live with me, and be my love,*
*and we will all the pleasures prove.*

**—Christopher Marlowe**

# I'll Be Rich!

## 29

## Having a Brilliant Idea

Eureka! You just came up with the most dazzling idea for a new product or service. Not only that, you've figured out some extraordinarily clever packaging and a catchy name as well. Now what?

**TEN**
things you
should know

1 **Who's going to buy it?** Having a great idea is exciting, but it's not enough. The single most important factor in commercializing any idea is its marketability. Before thinking about patents, lawyers, or licensing, do some research on potential purchasers of your product and how to reach them.

2 **No reservations.** You cannot reserve a patent at the U.S. Patent and Trademark Office (USPTO). However, you can file a provisional patent application (PPA) that will give you patent-pending status and preserve your place in line at the USPTO for at least one year.

3 **Keep it secret.** You don't need to operate like Fort Knox, but you should use reasonable methods of secrecy to protect your idea, such as nondisclosure agreements and labeling material "confidential."

4 **Patent protection ≠ money.** Half of U.S. patent applications are not granted. Of the ones that are, fewer then 3% are turned into commercial products.

5 **No trade, no trademark.** You cannot obtain federal trademark or service mark registration until you offer the product or service for sale. However, you can reserve a trademark if you genuinely intend to use it within a certain period of time.

**6** **Search and (with luck) you will not find.** Just because you've never seen it in a store, doesn't mean it hasn't been invented. You can't get a patent if someone had the same idea before you and applied for a patent already. Search the patent office records at www.uspto.gov and, if necessary, hire a professional patent searcher.

**7** **Careful what you wish for.** Getting a patent, trademark, or copyright doesn't guarantee you anything except the right to go after people who rip off your idea. You still have to chase down infringers, and that means legal fees and hassles.

**8** **Is it feasible?** Anyone interested in licensing your product idea is going to ask what it will cost to manufacture. If the cost per unit is higher than competing products, you're unlikely to make a deal—no matter how great your idea.

**9** **Watch out for deductions.** If you do enter into a licensing deal, pay attention to royalties, but also watch out for a long list of deductions that the licensing manufacturer will make before calculating your royalties.

**10** **It's not about one great idea.** Successful inventors always come up with many ideas. That's why they're successful. If your first great idea isn't marketable, don't fret … there are more where that came from.

*Why didn't I think of that?* Yes, the USPTO has granted patents for:

- a reservation system for using airplane restrooms (US 6,329,919)

- a wind-assisted bicycle (US 6,932,368)

- a vest with tubing so your hamster can crawl around in your clothing (US 5,901,666)

- a chewable toothbrush (US 6,769,828)

- a kissing shield (US 6,789,799)

- a plow that can also be used as a gun (US 35,600)

- a fireplace that includes a waterfall (US 6,901,925)

- a device that freezes dog poop (US 6,883,462) (Did you ever see the movie *Envy*? The product that makes its inventor rich is "Vapoorize.")

- a combination lawn/garden ornament and cremation container (US 6,854,165)

# Rock on . . .

30

## Starting a Band

Wow, it sure is great to plug your guitar into
an amp and rock out with your pals. But
whether you're putting a band together with
friends or building a band with strangers,
here are some things to know.

1 **Was that two large and a medium?** The major source of income for most touring bands is t-shirt sales. Yes, music matters, but when it comes to band business, merchandise rocks the cash register.

2 **"But I only care about music."** Somebody in the band has to manage the deals and money. Unless one band member wants to stay on top of the business … you won't have any business.

3 **The money is in the songs.** Songwriting members of successful bands usually earn twice as much (or more) than non-songwriting members.

4 **When harmony isn't sweet.** The two most common reasons ex-band members sue each other for are ownership of the band name and songwriting income.

5 **Protect yourself.** You don't have to do anything to get copyright other than "record" your song in some way, whether in audio, on paper, or in your computer (you're not protected if it is just in your head). Copyright is automatic in the U.S. (But you get extra rights if you file a copyright registration with the U.S. Copyright Office: www.copyright.gov.)

6 **No free lunch.** For some people, there is no such thing as a permissible sampling. According to one federal court, use of a two-second sample was copyright infringement.

**7  Forget CD sales and iTunes.** The fastest-growing source of income for musicians is downloadable ring tones.

**8  Write it down.** The single most effective way to avoid business squabbles among band members is to create a partnership agreement. An informal (but written) agreement explaining equipment ownership interests, music publishing, and rights to the band name will solve most potential band problems.

**9  "Everything was great until we signed the record deal."** Often it's not what's in the contract but who you're signing the contract with. Thousands of indie bands and their labels were left penniless because they put all their distribution in the hands of one company—Rough Trade—which went bankrupt in 1990.

**10  "You want a piece of me?"** Watch out for managers and attorneys who want part of your music publishing revenue. If they don't have a track record or you're just starting out with them, check them out carefully before signing away your songs. Ask for evidence of their efforts in music publishing, speak with any other bands or musicians that the manager or attorney has represented in the past, and Google them to see if they've been in disputes over similar issues.

## It Sure Goes Fast

Musicians who filed for bankruptcy after having a hit: **Meat Loaf** (after selling 20 million copies), **Toni Braxton** (who lost millions in bad deals), rap star **Luther Campbell** (who gave up a 36-hole golf course), **Tom Petty** (after hassles with his label), **George Clinton** (faced with a lawsuit), and **Mick Fleetwood**.

Musicians with tax problems: **Marvin Gaye** (who left the country briefly) and **Jerry Lee Lewis** (who didn't receive royalty payments for over a decade). And let's not forget **Ray Sawyer**, aka **Dr. Hook**, whose band's first album after emerging from bankruptcy court was titled "Bankrupt."

# Wedding Fever

## 31

### When You Become Engaged

After someone pops the question, there are a myriad of other questions to be answered. Here are some things to consider as you move toward the big event.

1. **It's all in the family.** If either of you already has children, ask for their blessing and involve them in the ceremony. Discuss child-rearing responsibilities and the possibility of adoption before you say "I do."

2. **Consider eloping**. If your families are offering to foot the bill, ask them to instead put the money towards a down payment on a house or in an educational savings account. Then throw a big party and order pizzas (very good pizzas, of course)!

3. **This won't happen to you, but ....** In the case of a broken engagement, who keeps the ring? In some states, such as Missouri and Kansas, an engagement ring is a gift, pure and simple. In other states, such as New York and New Mexico, the ring is a conditional gift. If the marriage doesn't happen, the ring belongs to the giver. In still other states, such as Texas and Washington, the ring goes to the person who was not at fault in breaking the engagement.

4. **The big event.** Sundays and winter months are less popular for weddings, and venues are often much less expensive then.

5. **It's true.** Many ceremony and reception venues require wedding insurance to cover them for possible injuries—during that extremely dangerous bouquet toss, for example. Ask your homeowners' or renters' insurance agent to add a wedding insurance rider to your current policy.

31 Your Little Legal Companion

**6** **Money talk—the ultimate intimacy.** Clarify property ownership and responsibility for debts each of you bring into the marriage. The best way to do this is with a prenuptial agreement.

**7** **Wedding World.** Any good or service with the word "wedding" attached costs more money. When planning, try finding providers outside the industry, such as "event photographers" instead of "wedding photographers."

**8** **There might be a catch.** If your parents offer to pay for the event, that money is a gift, not a contract that you'll plan a wedding and reception per their wishes. Interest in family peace may dictate otherwise, however.

**9** **Relax for a moment.** Keeping your engagement secret for a while allows you to enjoy the momentous decision. Soon enough you will be fending off a barrage of questions about your big news: "When?" "Where?" "Where are you registered?" "Where are you going on your honeymoon?"

**10** **Go on a honeymoon!** You may be exhausted, and your cash may be strapped to the limit, but find a way to get away—even if it's a tent in the woods.

## The Vein of What?

Engagement rings have always been worn on the third
finger (or fourth if you call the thumb a finger) of the left
hand. The ancient Romans and other early civilizations
believed this finger was the beginning of the vena amoris
("vein of love"), the vein that leads directly to the heart.

# What to Know Before "I Do"

**32**

## Getting Married

Couples planning marriage can easily get caught up in the wedding details, fraught with conflicting expectations from multiple parties. All of the wedding business can obscure that fact that getting married has big-time legal consequences and actually changes your rights and responsibilities as an individual. Listen up!

**TEN**
things you
should know

• • • • • • • • • • ▶

1 **"Prenup" is not a dirty word.** Everyone who's getting married should at least consider making a prenuptial agreement, if only to have a conversation about whether they want to keep any of their premarital property separate or not.

2 **Oh, wait—are you already married?** Common law marriage occurs when a state treats a long-term relationship essentially like a marriage, even though there's been no ceremony. However, it exists only in a few states, and according to pretty strict rules. Check with a lawyer if you think you're in one.

3 **It's all about the paperwork.** Every state requires that you get a marriage license before you say "I do," but each state varies in its requirements for getting the license. In some, you just hand over some money; in others, you must have medical tests done.

4 **Church vs. state.** Civil marriage is when you are legally married in the eyes of the state. All marriages in the U.S. are civil marriages, because they require a civil license in order to be valid. You can also enter into a religious marriage by having a religious ceremony, but that's not what makes you married according to the state.

5 **It's not just about you anymore.** After you are married, you are required to support your spouse and any children that you have during your marriage. You also have the right, among others, to make medical decisions for your spouse if he or she isn't able to make them.

6   **His, hers, and ours.** Property that you had before you were
    married doesn't necessarily become jointly owned once you're
    married. Different states treat spouses' property differently. If you
    have property that you want to keep separate, see a lawyer before
    you get married.

7   **In 49 states, it's only a man and a woman.** In Massachusetts,
    same-sex couples may legally marry.

8   **Other states of the union.** California, Connecticut, Hawaii,
    Maine, New Jersey, and Vermont all have laws that provide for
    marriage-like relationships—either domestic partnerships or civil
    unions.

9   **Marriage, schmarriage.** Although there are well over two
    million marriages a year in the U.S., only 52.1% of adult females
    and 52.6% of adult males were married (and not separated) in
    2000, according to the U.S. Census.

10  **"I do" sometimes doesn't mean forever.** More than half of
    first marriages end in divorce, and over 65% of second marriages
    do. If you're on the fence about getting married, don't do it! And
    lots of experts recommend premarital counseling to make sure
    you're really compatible.

Getting Married   32

*"I love being married. It's so great to find that one special person you want to annoy for the rest of your life."*

—**Rita Rudner**

# Congratulations!

**33**

## You Want to Run a Marathon

The idea of running a marathon may sound like torture to you, in which case you should move quickly onto the next section. If you are a hardy soul who is considering this adventure, however, here are the following pointers.

1 **Take your time.** Allow nine months to a year to prepare, less if you already run 20 to 35 miles per week. Still want to do this?

2 **Pick thoughtfully.** If you're seeking your fastest time, choose a relatively flat course with cool temperatures (40 to 50 degrees). Do you want breathtaking views? Do crowds excite or agitate you? Think about the experience you want and choose your race accordingly.

3 **Write down a plan.** Calculate your mileage goals and workout schedule at least one month ahead. For help, there are lots of books, magazines, and online resources with good programs for all different levels.

4 **If the shoes fit ... buy them.** Explain your needs and previous foot or shoe problems to a knowledgeable salesperson. Once you find something you like, buy two pairs, and make sure you have a relatively new (although not brand-new) pair for race day.

5 **Find training partners.** Company can make a two-hour training run fly by (okay, maybe not fly by, but go faster). And guilt will get you out the door on rainy, dark, cold days when you know someone is waiting. If you don't have running buddies already, ask your local sports store about clubs.

 Your Little Legal Companion

**6** **Hydrate, hydrate, hydrate.** Don't run longer than an hour without water. Sports drinks help prevent overheating and dehydration, but you'll need to experiment with what fluids, gels, sports bars, and other supplements will work for you on race day. Another skill to develop? Drinking while running!

**7** **Listen to your body.** Consider this as important in your training as any of your runs. Get the extra rest and food you'll need as you increase your mileage and training. Otherwise you risk getting run down, sick, or injured. End result? No marathon.

**8** **What about that stabbing pain?** Heroic Olympic tales are for inspiration, not imitation. Don't stick to your running plan if you are limping down the stairs to get out the door. If you experience pain, back off for a few days. If there's no improvement, have it checked out.

**9** **Keep it fun.** This is a hobby, not a job. Make sure you enjoy the process. Vary your runs, find running friends, treat yourself to naps and ice cream.

**10** **Don't race to the race.** If you're traveling somewhere, get there a day or two ahead of time, allowing you to start the race relaxed, prepared, and focused on meeting this amazing challenge.

You Want to Run a Marathon    33

*Success is a journey, not a destination.*
*The doing is usually more important*
*than the outcome.*

**—Arthur Ashe**

# When Baby Makes Three

34

## Having a Child

Having a child—by either birth or adoption—is a life-changing event. And once you get used to chronic sleep deprivation, it's really quite fun! Here are some tips for the practical side of things.

**TEN**
things you
should know

● ● ● ● ● ● ● ● ● ● ▶

1 **Health insurance is not created equal.** You've already experienced it in other areas, but it goes double for pregnancy. Make sure yours adequately covers prenatal and maternity care (if your employer has 15 or more employees, federal law says it must); the type of delivery you want (not all plans cover delivery at birth centers); and pediatric visits and immunizations.

2 **Too bad there's no law mandating sleep.** Federal law (the Family and Medical Leave Act) gives many workers 12 weeks of unpaid leave to care for a newborn. Some employers and some states give better benefits; California, for example, mandates a short amount of paid leave.

3 **Consider an epidural.** If you're expecting for the first time, many mothers recommend it. If this is the second time, you probably know for yourself. (We're not really offering medical advice.)

4 **Baby's first credit card.** Just kidding, but you should get a Social Security number for your baby right away. The hospital will probably provide the form. You'll need the number to claim child-related tax breaks, add your baby to insurance policies, and set up a college savings or bank account for your child.

5 **You thought you had a lot of luggage.** Pound for pound, those little people sure have a lot of stuff. Make sure the crib, stroller, and other products you buy are safe (look for the Juvenile Products Manufacturers seal of approval and read Consumer Reports).

 Your Little Legal Companion

**6** **Leroy, cover your eyes.** If you're breastfeeding, you have a legal right to feed your baby in public and to express breast milk at work. (In California, Minnesota, and a few other states, employers must make reasonable efforts to provide a private space for this.)

**7** **Uncle Sam loves kids.** As a parent, you get tax breaks, such as a dependent exemption and a child tax credit. There are also special tax breaks for adoptive parents. See www.irs.gov.

**8** **Mary Poppins, please.** If you'll need child care, start looking for a nanny, day care center, or home-based provider at least several months before you need someone. Start with the parent grapevine (friends, neighbors, work colleagues, even your pediatrician's office) and local parenting websites. Always do a thorough screening and reference check.

**9** **If you don't have a will, now's the time.** And if you do have a will, now's the time to change it. In it, name a guardian— someone you trust to raise your child in the unlikely event that someday you can't.

**10** **Enjoy every minute!** All the clichés are true—they really do grow up fast.

## *What's in a name?*

Emily has been the most popular girl's name in the U.S. for the past ten years.

Famous Emilys include:

- **Emily Dickinson**, poet

- **Emily Post**, etiquette expert

- **Emily Bronte**, author (*Wuthering Heights*)

- **Emily Litella**, Gilda Radner character ("Never mind") on Saturday Night Live in the 1970s

- **Emily Watson**, actress (*Punch-Drunk Love*)

- **Emily the Strange**, 13-year-old counter-culture character with four black cats seen on everything from t-shirts and bags to shoes

- **Emily** is also the name of a small town in Minnesota and a strong hurricane in 2005.

# Growing Your Family

**35**

## Adopting a Child

Few decisions in life require more thought and a greater commitment than adopting a child. Whether you already have other children or are adopting your first child, you should know a few things before you start the process.

**TEN**
things you
should know

1 **Lots of kids need loving homes**. Many children are available for domestic adoption, especially if you don't insist on an infant or are willing to take sibling groups or children of color.

2 **Know your terms.** In an "agency" adoption, an agency you hire helps match you with a birth mother, then assists with the legal aspects of the adoption. In an "independent" adoption, you find the birth mother yourself or with an adoption facilitator, and a private lawyer helps do the legal work. In a "kinship" adoption, you adopt the child of a relative. In an "open" adoption, you agree to maintain contact with the child's birth family, meaning anything from sending photos once a year to more frequent contact.

3 **Going overseas.** When U.S. parents adopt outside the U.S., most of the children come from China, Guatemala, Eastern Europe, or Cambodia.

4 **Your child is your child is your child.** An adopted child and a natural child are exactly the same in the eyes of the law. But not always in the eyes of a will or a trust. If your adopted child stands to inherit under a will or trust, make sure the document specifies that adopted children are included.

5 **Marriage doesn't make it so.** Stepparents are not legal parents of their partners' children unless they have legally adopted the children.

6 **An irrevocable decision.** When a child is adopted, generally the birth parents' rights are terminated forever. One possible exception to this is where the birth father didn't know that he had a child, and the adoption was completed without his consent. In some of those cases, the adoption might be revoked, but it's not automatic—the judge would look at all the circumstances.

7 **It's never too late to have a happy childhood.** Adults can be adopted, too. All it takes is an agreement between the two adults. In some states, the adopting parent must be older than the person being adopted by a certain amount (in California, for example, it's 10 years).

8 **Privacy still matters here.** Although most court proceedings are a matter of public record, adoption files are not.

9 **All over the map.** Same-sex couples can adopt in many states, but not all. Florida bans adoption of all kinds for lesbians and gay men. Living in a state that allows you to enter into a marriage-like relationship with your same-sex partner, such as California or Vermont, doesn't necessarily protect parental rights completely. In those states, even if one partner is the biological parent, the non-biological parent should still probably do an adoption.

10 **Not to put a price on it, but . . . .** Adoption expenses can range from minimal in a simple proceeding like a stepparent adoption, to many tens of thousands of dollars in an international adoption.

Adopting a Child 35

*Children make your life important.*

—**Erma Bombeck**

# I'm Not Ready!

36

## When Your Child Starts Kindergarten

One minute your child is teething, and the next she is supposed to start school. Entering kindergarten is a big step for a child, and perhaps a bigger one for the parents! You can help get your child off to a good start by keeping a few things in mind.

**TEN**
things you
should know

• • • • • • • • • ▶

1 **Don't rush it.** If you don't think your child is emotionally or socially ready for kindergarten, and your pediatrician and preschool teacher agree, wait a year.

2 **Prepare yourself.** Find out the school rules and procedures, including the required forms and immunizations, daily schedule and school year calendar, food services, and opportunities for parent involvement. Starting at least three to six months before school begins will help keep you from feeling frantic.

3 **Prepare your child.** Visit the school over the summer to see the classroom and playground. Read your child Miss Bindergarten Gets Ready for Kindergarten, by Joseph Slate. Encourage your child to ask the teacher about any questions or concerns—whether it's where the bathroom is or what to bring for sharing time.

4 **Be brave.** Tears always flow the first day of kindergarten. Sometimes the children cry, too. Try not to be weepy (or at least wait until you get to the car).

5 **Speak up.** Let the teacher and school know about your child's allergies or other health concerns. And if your child can't bring his favorite sandwich—peanut butter—because of a classmate's peanut allergies, take the time to explain why to him.

**6** **Relax about "academics."** Don't worry if your five-year-old can't read yet; she'll be glued to Harry Potter before you know it. There's plenty of time to stress about schoolwork and college admissions.

*Check out www.parentcenter.com for useful articles on kindergarten.*

**7** **Attend parent-teacher conferences.** Several states give parents the right to miss a certain number of work hours because of their children's school activities. These states include California, the District of Columbia, Illinois, Louisiana, Massachusetts, Minnesota, Nevada, North Carolina, Rhode Island, and Vermont.

**8** **Keep germs at home.** Don't make your kids miserable (and infect everyone else) by sending them to school when they're ill. You have the legal right to use your sick leave to care for a sick child in at least three states (California, Minnesota, and Washington).

**9** **Ask for help if you need it.** If your child might have a learning difficulty, get the teacher's opinion and ask about an Individualized Education Program (IEP). You have the right to get your child assessed for the need for special education services such as speech or occupational therapy.

**10** **Enjoy it while you can.** Before you know it, you'll have a teenager who won't want to be seen with you.

## Give Kids a Break

*Teddy Bear, Teddy Bear, turn around*

*Teddy Bear, Teddy Bear, touch the ground*

*Teddy Bear, Teddy Bear, show your shoe*

*Teddy Bear, Teddy Bear, that will do!*

**—Popular children's jump rope rhyme**

Ask any kid their favorite part of school, and it will probably be recess—those oh-too-brief breaks kids have to jump rope, play tag, or just swap the latest trading cards or silly jokes with friends. Unfortunately, many schools have abolished recess, because of safety and liability concerns and pressure to provide more classroom time. For advice on saving recess in your child's school, check out the American Association for the Child's Right to Play at www.ipausa.org. And if you just want to relive recess, see www.gameskidsplay.net for hundreds of playground games and jump rope rhymes.

# Breaking Up
# Is Hard to Do

## 37

## What You Should Know
## About Divorce

Unfortunately, it happens to a lot of marriages.
If you are thinking about splitting with your
mate or your spouse has walked out, do some
research on your options. There are ways to
keep the pain of the divorce procedure to
a minimum. Get help from friends, family,
counselors. Most important, know that you
will survive this difficult process.

**TEN**
things you
should know

1 **Spying isn't necessary.** Every state has no-fault divorce, so you can get a divorce based on "irreconcilable differences" or the like. You do not have to prove adultery or other offenses. However, some states still consider the concept of fault when making decisions about child custody or alimony.

2 **Shopping for divorce court.** Every state has a residency requirement, meaning you have to live there for a certain amount of time before filing for divorce. Nevada has the shortest at six weeks—that's why people go there for "quickie divorces."

3 **"We definitely made a mistake."** If you've only been married a short time and don't have kids or much property, you can usually get a "summary divorce." You and your spouse file jointly, and the process is expedited.

4 **Solomon's choice.** Most courts prefer to order shared or joint custody of children. If a court must decide who gets primary custody, one of several factors considered is which parent will likely be more supportive of the children's relationship with the other parent.

5 **It's not over till it's over.** Every state has a waiting period between filing your divorce papers and the date you get a divorce judgment. Anyone who has ever watched All My Children knows, you can't get married again until your divorce is final.

 Your Little Legal Companion

**6** **Yippee, you get a lawyer, too.** In a few states, you can't represent yourself in a divorce—you have to have a lawyer file papers for you.

**7** **Reach for your wallet.** The average American wedding costs $22,000. The average contested American divorce can cost about the same, and if the conflict goes all the way to a trial, costs can top $70,000.

**8** **Quicker, cheaper, less pain.** In divorce mediation, a neutral third person (the mediator) works with the couple to help them decide custody, support, and division of property. The couple can then file an uncontested divorce and move on.

**9** **Another high road.** Collaborative divorce is also preferable: You and your spouse each have lawyers, but everyone signs a "no court" agreement and decides the issues together. If you can't resolve your divorce, you start again with a new lawyer. This expensive consequence provides incentive to resolve things through a collaborative process.

**10** **Kids first, feelings second.** Your kids will suffer less if you don't fight over them, don't talk about the other parent negatively, and handle the divorce quickly and cooperatively. Tell your friends, not your children, how lousy your ex is.

## *Aversion Therapy—It Works!*

Here are two ways to lessen your chances of getting divorced: (1) choose your mate carefully, and (2) sit down with a pint of ice cream and a DVD of *Kramer vs. Kramer* or *The War of the Roses*. That should do it.

# Bon Voyage

## 38

### Going on Your Dream Trip

The most important tip we can give about a dream trip is: *Don't forget to take it!* Kids, school, work, pets, home—our commitments keep us busy and in the same place, but if you have a dream destination, it is never too early to start thinking and planning. Once you're committed to your trip, here are a few travel tips.

**TEN**
things you
should know

• • • • • • • • ▶

1   **Are your documents in order?** If you're leaving the country, you need a current passport, even for Mexico or Canada. You might need a visa, too. Check www.travel.state.gov to find exactly what you need to enter the country of your choice—and to get back into this one. Start several months ahead to get it all done.

2   **Remember travelers' cheques?** Leave them at home. ATMs are the fastest and easiest way to get money abroad. Your bank calculates the conversion, and you get the cash you need in the local currency. Before you leave, however, make sure your PIN will work and find out what fees (if any) are charged for international withdrawals. Oh, and don't forget your ATM card.

3   **What did you say?** That hand gesture of yours may not translate around the world. For instance, in some parts of South America, what we know as the a-okay sign is a serious insult! Take a little time to research the local customs—it could save you considerable, shall we say, discomfort.

4   **Did we mention "research"?** While you're becoming an expert on local custom, pay attention to local laws as well. As much as we all have learned about U.S. law from Law and Order marathons, it is the laws of the country you're visiting that count. And they may not be so friendly.

**5** **If you find trouble (or trouble finds you), put your tax dollars to work and call Uncle Sam.** Before leaving home, figure out which U.S. embassy or consulate serves your travel destination (www.travel.state.gov), read its consulate sheet, and take the local phone number with you.

**6** **The ultimate comfort item?** Toilet paper. An extra roll and some hand sanitizer can address most unmentionable hygiene issues. You'll especially appreciate these after your third night of sleeping in train stations.

**7** **Don't forget to write.** The local Internet café may be your lifeline to home, but there's nothing like sending (and receiving) an old-fashioned postcard with a real foreign stamp and postmark.

**8** **Where's the Pepto?** Your stomach may not be ready for foreign bugs. Taste the local fare with caution, and bring plenty of your favorite intestinal recovery medicine—just in case.

**9** **Last-minute step.** Before leaving, check the U.S. international travel advisory list. Landing in the middle of a coup may not be the dream vacation you had in mind.

**10** **Don't worry about Fideau.** He'll miss you while you're gone, he'll be happy when you get back, and you will be forgiven. Really.

Going on Your Dream Trip  38

You might be surprised what this
gesture means in Ecuador!

# It's Not for Sissies

39

## Getting Old

Suddenly, it hits you—you're old. Well, at least you're *older*. You wake up and your arms are too short for reading the newspaper. The upside? You get a discount at the movies (as if there were any you wanted to see). There's no stopping aging, so you might as well start taking care of yourself, mentally, financially, and physically.

**TEN**
things you
should know

1 **Active brains live longer.** Consider Supreme Court justices: Since the Court began functioning in 1789, over 50% of the more than 100 justices have served into at least their middle 70s. Remember that more than half of those justices died before 1900, when average U.S. life expectancy was less than 50 years!

2 **Feeling bad is not normal.** Depression was previously viewed as a natural part of the aging process. Now health professionals see it as a treatable disease, and may deal with it in various ways. Get help if you need it.

3 **Remember Terry Schiavo.** Making a health care directive (a "living will") is essential if you want your wishes followed regarding artificially prolonged life support. Equally important? Your loved ones knowing where the document is located.

4 **Worried someone will challenge your will?** Unlikely. Legal challenges rarely occur. When they do, the challenger must prove that the document is technically improper, you were of unsound mind when creating it (courts assume the opposite), or you signed the document through fraud or under duress—all very tough to prove legally.

5 **Feeling discriminated against?** If you're over 40 (yes, that means you're old) and were discriminated against in an employment relationship because of your age (whether in an interview, at termination, or regarding your retirement benefits), you may have a claim under federal law.

6   **But what about that yogurt?** Only about 50 people in human history have been documented as reaching the age of 114. Only one person indisputably lived to 120.

7   **What retirement?** In a recent study by University of Minnesota researcher Jan Hively, about 40% of seniors interviewed said they worked after retirement age (half because they had to and half because they wanted to), and most planned to do so until physically unable.

8   **Living longer and stronger.** Fewer than five percent of people over 65 are in nursing homes, and the figure is dropping. People are healthier, and alternative living arrangements (such as assisted living residences, where residents have their own apartments and can choose from a smorgasbord of services) are mushrooming.

9   **Want to avoid probate?** Payable-on-death bank accounts (PODs) offer one easy way. All you do is complete a simple form provided by your bank, naming the person who inherits the money in the account at your death.

10  **We've heard a rumor that exercise is good for you.** Have you heard it, too?

Getting Old   39

| Age-related Topic | Best Movie About It |
|---|---|
| Fantasizing about youth | *Cocoon* (1985)<br>Seniors swim in a magic pool and find themselves energized. |
| The down sides of retirement | *About Schmidt* (2002)<br>Retired exec sets off for misadventures in his oversized vehicle. |
| Old people fighting mummies | *Bubba Ho Tep* (2002)<br>Elvis and JFK, both alive and in nursing homes, fight for their fellow residents. |
| Settling scores | *The Straight Story* (1996)<br>An old man journeys by tractor to mend his relationship with an ill brother. |
| Old man and felines | *Harry and Tonto* (1974)<br>A retired teacher travels the country with his cat. |

# Stormy Weather

## Surviving a Natural Disaster

Did you know over three times as many people die worldwide from natural disasters as from political conflict? Although there's often little to be done the moment the forces of nature strike, common sense and preparation can make a difference.

1 **What disaster should you worry about?** It depends on your area. Wildfires, tsunamis, volcanoes, earthquakes, landslides, hurricanes, and tornadoes all strike the U.S., but the most common disaster is flooding. For flood protection, keep sandbags, plywood, plastic sheeting, and garbage bags on hand.

2 **Should you "go bare," that is, not carry special catastrophic coverage?** That depends on how well your home is fortified against the disaster, and whether you live in a high-risk area, are already carrying heavy debt, and can access money quickly after a calamity (such as through a home equity line). In case of calamity, are you prepared to give up your ruined home and move to another area?

3 **We all hate to do it, but read your policy (and keep a copy elsewhere).** In a disaster, an insurer may attempt to apply multiple deductibles for a single claim. That's usually prohibited unless the property was damaged by multiple disasters.

4 **And another thing.** Your insurance policy should not only cover your living expenses during a natural disaster when you're forced to leave your home, but also during its repair.

5 **Deal relief.** If a natural disaster prevents you from fulfilling your end of a business deal, your written contract may help. Look for a "Force Majeure" or "Acts of God" provision, which may allow you to delay performance until the disaster is under control.

6 **Nature knows nature.** Some people advise against holding your dog or cat during an earthquake—instead, trust it to follow instinct and find a safe place to hide. Another pet tip: Most disaster shelters cannot take pets due to health regulations.

*For more preparedness tips, check out the website www.72hours.org.*

7 **More good news.** If your house was built before 1978, severe damage may unearth asbestos in its walls and ceiling. Have your home checked for asbestos (your insurance policy may cover this cost).

8 **Maybe California isn't so scary.** The number of geophysical disasters—earthquakes, landslides, eruptions—has remained steady over the past decade, but the number of hydro-meteorological disasters—droughts, windstorms, and floods—has more than doubled. In that decade, over 90% of those killed by natural disasters perished in hydro-meteorological events.

9 **Concerned about landslides?** Know the warning signs: cracks in plaster or tile, bulging ground at the base of a slope, tilting fences, or the noise of cracking trees.

10 **Rest easier.** No matter what natural disaster strikes your area, it's always wise to move beds away from the windows.

Surviving a Natural Disaster 40

| Natural Disaster | Best Book About It |
|---|---|
| Hurricane | *Isaac's Storm*, by Erik Larson. (America's deadliest natural disaster, the Galveston hurricane of 1900.) |
| Flood | *The Johnstown Flood*, by David McCullough. (The 1889 flood and subsequent national scandal.) |
| Earthquake | *A Crack in the Edge of the World*, by Simon Winchester. (The devastating 1906 San Francisco earthquake.) |
| Volcano | *Krakatoa,* by Simon Winchester. (The historic 1883 eruption and subsequent fundamentalist rampage.) |
| Wildfire | *Fire on the Mountain*, by John N. Maclean. (The catastrophic Colorado South Canyon fire of 1994.) |

# Did You Say Garage or Garbage?

## Holding the Best Garage Sale

There's a reason garage sales never go out of
style. We've all got too much stuff—but none
of us can resist a bargain, either. Sales offer
a satisfying way to reduce clutter or raise
money for a good cause. Kids enjoy taking
part, too.

**TEN**
things you
should know

1. **Big Brother.** Check with your local government whether any restrictions apply to your type of sale or to posting signs. You may need a sale permit.

2. **Think like Wal-Mart.** The more stuff you have to sell, the more people will show up. Consider combining your sale with other households.

3. **Getting the word out.** Websites such as Craigslist will place ads for free. Neighborhood signs with big, legible lettering will draw the largest crowds. (But remember to remove them later.)

4. **Price everything and price it to sell.** Some people will pass by an item if it isn't marked. The price should be lower than a thrift store's, unless your sale benefits a charitable cause. Then you should have a sign or pamphlets explaining where the dollars are going. If more than one household is involved, identify on the tag who owns the item so you can divvy up proceeds later.

5. **Get up early.** Like ants at a picnic, you can't keep early birds away. If your ads say "9 a.m.," you'll have people there at 8:30. Try roping the area off or threatening encroachers with a water hose (this never works), or just relax and start selling.

6. **Have on hand:** Cash box. Calculator.  Plenty of empty bags and newspaper or wrapping material. Lots of small bills and change (accept only cash). Bonus item? Use of a truck for delivering large items and toting the sale's leftovers to the Salvation Army.

**7** **Staff needed:** Brain (for minding the money), bargainer (for negotiating), and brawn (for loading and getting lunch). For multi-household or large sales, line up more volunteers than you think you'll need.

**8** **Mark your territory.** Delineate where the sale ends and your home begins. Otherwise, you might find someone in your kitchen, picking out new dishes.

**9** **Worried you'll later see your item on the Antiques Roadshow?** Unlikely, but take any questionable items to a local dealer for appraisal before the sale.

**10** **If in doubt, put it out.** Anything you don't want, someone will buy—half-used bottles of shampoo, cleaning products you don't like, scrap lumber, broken tiles, florist vases. A "Free" box will get some people to stop and look. Isn't it great that someone will use what you don't want?

## How Did It Start?

Although the garage sale now seems like a quintessentially American, free-market event, it actually didn't hit U.S. shores until the 1950s. The inspiration of French flea markets moved to the picket-fenced, expansive green lawns of the American suburbs. Both homeownership and consumer affluence were on the rise, and one could hear the first cries of "I've got too much stuff!" Nowadays, anything purchased at a 1950s garage sale—maybe a Betty Crocker cookbook, an early Slinky toy, or a Bakelite clock—has probably risen in value.

# The Next Stage

## Going Back to School

Whether you are determined to finish a degree you started long ago or to tackle another level of education, these tips may help in the transition.

1. **Test the water.** If money is tight or you simply aren't sure going back to school is for you, try auditing a local class. You'll probably need permission from the school administrative office and the professor, but many are happy to have you "try it out." And some universities let seniors audit classes for free.

2. **Financial aid?** It's a jungle out there. Assistance may come in the form of federal aid, state aid, or grants or fellowships that are school- or program-specific. Make friends with the financial aid officers at the schools you are considering. You'll need their guidance as you fight through the maze of paperwork and loan requirements.

3. **Peace at home.** Your family may not be thrilled with your decision to return to school. Help garner their support by involving them—talk about what you're learning, invite them to school, and thank them profusely when they do more around the house.

4. **Go away and learn.** If you're a student in your golden years, why not combine your education with travel? Consider the study abroad programs with Elderhostel (www.Elderhostel.org).

5. **Online makes it possible.** Online programs and courses allow you to listen to lectures, participate in live discussions, and take exams at times and locations that work for you. Investigate a program's legitimacy by comparing its curriculum and instructors to that of other programs, interviewing graduates, and asking people in the field about the program's reputation.

 Your Little Legal Companion

6    **Work it.** If you're seeking a degree, you may be able to apply credit you received for courses taken years ago, or use the knowledge to test out of lower-level classes. Don't forget your life experience, either. Talk with your department head about special study credit for projects you may be doing at work or elsewhere.

7    **Remember how clueless you were at 20?** The great thing about being an older student is that your goals are clearer, whether seeking knowledge, personal growth, fun, or earning power. Recognizing what you wish to accomplish will focus and enrich your school experience.

8    **Tax breaks, too.** Depending on your income, you may recognize some tax advantages from your new life as a coed. Check out the Lifetime Learning Credit, the Hope Credit, and student loan interest and tuition-related deductions.

9    **"Can I combine my senior and student discounts?"** Probably not. However, enjoy your student benefits—get in shape at the school gym, revel in discounted campus events, and take advantage of an affordable student health care plan.

10   **Plenty of people will tell you you are crazy to go back to school.** Remember, you are doing this for you. What better investment is there?

Going Back to School   42

*What was that about old dogs?*

Almost 85,000 men and women over 50 are full-time students in undergraduate or graduate programs, according to the U.S. Department of Education. There are another 435,000 part-time students.

# Ready to Polish That Halo?

**43**

## Feel Good by Doing Some Good

Whether you're 15 or 50, you may be inspired to help the world around you. Here's how you can make a difference in a rewarding way.

**1** **Resist doling out small amounts to lots of charities.** You'll find yourself on endless mailing lists, and your donations will get eaten up on postage asking you for more. Besides, donating larger amounts to one or two charities may increase your status. You may meet a celebrity or two. Isn't that what charity is all about?

**2** **Don't be thin-skinned.** If a charity is late thanking you for donating, or refers to you as "Mrs." rather than "Mr.," it's probably because they're focusing their limited resources on providing services.

**3** **Thinking of volunteering?** Why? No, really—why? Just like a job search, make sure your goals (meeting people, building skills, doing whatever is needed) match the volunteer opportunities of the charity. It's perfectly okay to ask the staff.

**4** **Roll up your sleeves.** Some think that serving on a nonprofit's board is an honorary position where you meet celebrities (see No. 1). In fact, board members must provide oversight and fundraise and are personally liable for any mismanagement.

**5** **Tax-exempt?** Tax-deductible? Know the difference. Unless an organization is a "501(c)(3)," you probably can't deduct your gift—despite the fact that the organization says it's tax-exempt (meaning it doesn't pay taxes).

 Your Little Legal Companion

6 **No free lunch.** If you get a gift for donating, or you buy an auction item, your tax deduction is reduced by the value of the item (unless it truly is a token). For donations of $250 or more, charities must provide a receipt, including the estimated value of the item.

7 **Be a savvy contributor.** Check out charities whose work you don't know personally using websites like www.guidestar.org or www.charitywatch.org.

8 **Leaving a gift to charity in your will?** Don't add lots of restrictions, like "I leave my house on the condition that it shelter albino squirrels." The charity may decline the gift.

9 **You know this, but . . . .** Don't give cash, and never give your credit card number or other personal details to a phone solicitor from an unknown organization.

10 **Get your kids into the giving habit.** Raise their allowance, with the extra cash set aside for an end-of-year charitable gift. Then help them choose a worthy charity.

Feel Good by Doing Some Good 43

*Celebrity Items You've Already Missed Your Chance to Buy at a Charity Auction:*

- Gillian Anderson's flip flops (autographed!)

- Alice Cooper's golf clubs

- Couture Roberto Cavalli gown worn by Britney Spears

- James Brown's sunglasses

- Ellen DeGeneres's Grammy Award sneakers

- Self portrait by comedienne Phyllis Diller

- Badge worn by Jack Lord on television series *Hawaii Five-O*

- Autographed John Tesh CD, *A Deeper Faith I*

- *Guide to 10 Downing Street* signed by Tony Blair

# Time Out

## When You Decide to Live in Another Country

If you are between jobs, just graduating, or starting your retirement, you may feel the urge to Do Something Completely Different. Whether working for an overseas agency or independently setting up your home away from home, there are a few things to consider.

**TEN**
things you
should know

● ● ● ● ● ● ● ● ●

1 **Follow the rules!** You are subject to the laws of your host country, and if you violate the law or the terms of your immigration status, you could be deported or, worse, imprisoned.

2 **Mind your body.** Update your vaccines, know what new diseases and conditions you'll be exposed to, and locate the best medical resources (quality can vary widely). If you have a U.S. health insurance policy, your plan may provide no coverage or require you to pay medical expenses out of pocket and apply for reimbursement.

3 **Travel light.** Visit before moving or find temporary housing before all your possessions arrive. Then figure out where you want to reside, what locals pay, and how local housing laws and customs work.

4 **Hello. Goodbye. Thank you. Where? How much?** If you like to travel, you know that learning even a few phrases in the local language expresses respect and is your first step to fluency. Read up on the country's culture, economy, politics, and history, too.

5 **Pay your taxes!** Even while living abroad, you must continue to pay U.S. income taxes. In countries that have a tax treaty with the U.S., the IRS will even be notified of your whereabouts. There's no escape.

6 **Fluffy—in jail?** Local laws may limit your ability to bring household pets or impose quarantines. Don't forget about your eventual return. U.S. laws may limit reentry.

7 **The joy of online banking.** Research the access you'll have to bank, investment, and retirement accounts from your new locale. If you can't or don't want to manage your finances online, you'll need to sign a power of attorney authorizing someone in the U.S. to handle your financial matters—it's up to you to decide whether your trust your brother more than online banking.

8 **Cover the bases.** Copy all your important records: recent financial documents such as bank statements and insurance policies as well as travel documents such as your birth certificate, passport, and visa. Take a copy with you and leave one with someone at home; you may need them in a pinch. Figure out where to receive mail in your new locale.

9 **Tell creditors you are leaving.** Order a credit report and send letters to all your creditors, insurance companies and health care providers. Notify the post office of a change of address and cancel magazine and newspaper subscriptions.

10 **On the home front.** There are people and things that you'll miss. Even while you're busy preparing your departure, be sure to enjoy that last meal at the local sushi bar or a picnic with your extended family.

*Twenty years from now you will be more disappointed by the things you didn't do than by the ones you did do. So throw off the bowlines, sail away from the safe harbor. Catch the trade winds in your sails. Explore. Dream. Discover.*

**—Mark Twain**

*If you actually look like your passport photo, you aren't well enough to travel.*

**—Sir Vivian Fuchs**

# Where's the Fire?

## Traffic Tickets

You hear the siren and you see the police officer motioning for you to pull over. Uh-oh .... We've included some things to keep in mind as the officer pulls out the citation book.

**TEN**
things you
should know
• • • • • • • • •

1 **Hate those red light cameras?** Nevertheless, they've been shown to reduce red light-running violations by about 40%. Still not impressed? Consider that about one out of ten accidents involve red light running and that motorists (and occupants) are more likely to be injured in these accidents than in other types of crashes.

2 **Just don't tick him (her) off.** If it's legal to have a radar detector in your car, and it is (except in Virginia and the District of Columbia), why do so many people hide them? Because most drivers believe they're more likely to be ticketed if an officer sees the device in the car.

3 **No gray area.** Most states have absolute speed limits; that is, one mile over the speed limit violates the law. You'll have only three defenses: attack how your speed was determined, claim you were forced to exceed the limit to avoid serious injury, or say the officer mistook you for another.

4 **There's only one correct answer.** If you're asked, "Do you know how fast you were going?" or "Do you know why you were pulled over?," say, "No." Let the officer show you were speeding, not the other way around.

5 **If you get a ticket following an accident, don't plead guilty.** If anyone involved in the accident sues you for damages, your admission of guilt could be used against you.

**6** **Fighting a ticket may be easier than you think.** If you show up for a court date and the ticketing officer doesn't, the ticket is usually tossed.

**7** **Air attack.** If you challenge a ticket for speeding detected by aircraft, you can ask that each of the air and ground officers be excluded from the courtroom while the other is testifying (preventing them from "remembering" based on each other's testimony). If the aircraft officer targeted many cars simultaneously, he might not recall if your car was one of them without the ground officer's verification.

**8** **Traffic school ain't what it used to be.** In many states you can wipe your record clean by attending comedy, online, or even pay-only-if-you-pass traffic schools.

**9** **No way out.** If you can't challenge your ticket and traffic school isn't an option, you can probably expect a hike in your insurance rates. To save money, you may want to revisit your policy and consider alternatives such as higher deductibles.

**10** **On the bright side.** Be glad you didn't get your traffic citation in Finland. There, traffic fines are proportional to a driver's income. Fines as high as $100,000 can be leveled on wealthy offenders.

## Some People Have Too Much Money

True story: A California Highway Patrol Officer pulled over a new Porsche going 120 miles per hour down a barren stretch of California freeway. To his surprise, the driver greeted him enthusiastically. "I'm trying to join a Porsche club, and I have to get a ticket going at least 100 miles per hour," the driver explained. "I've been driving up and down California, trying to get pulled over!"

The officer gave him a ticket—for 99 miles per hour.

# He Cheated Me!

## Going to Small Claims Court

Life offers many irritating and costly moments. Your neighbor backs over your beautiful maple tree: $500. Your customer refuses to pay his bill: $2,000. Your mechanic charges you to repair your car and the next day it dies: $1,000. When you are convinced that someone owes you money, but not so much that you want to hire a lawyer, small claims court may be the answer.

**TEN**
things you
should know

• • • • • • • • • • ▶

1 **Leveling the playing field.** Most small claims court participants represent themselves, so you probably won't be up against a lawyer.

2 **Small means "smallish."** Small claims courts have a dollar ceiling amount for claims, usually $2,500–$10,000. If your claim exceeds the maximum, you may still want to use this court to get what you can, rather than spending money and time on a lawyer and formal court proceedings.

3 **Try negotiating first.** Write a polite, businesslike letter explaining why the person owes you money. State that if you don't hear back by a specific date, you'll file a small claims case. To keep the tone right, assume that your letter will be read out loud in court. (You can use the letter to help prove your good faith.) And you heard it here first: Use plain English!

4 **Written evidence helps your case.** Bring to court evidence that supports your claim, such as letters, receipts, or even your notes of a conversation.

5 **Winning is one thing;** collecting is another. If the person you're suing has a job or real estate, you can either garnish their wages or put a lien on their property. If, however, the person is penniless, unemployed, and likely to stay that way, you may be wasting your time going to court.

**6**    **Which small claims court?** Court rules dictate where you can file your case. Generally, you're on solid ground if you sue where the defendant lives or works or where the dispute arose.

**7**    **Such a deal!** It doesn't cost much to file a small claims case. However, if your income is low and every dollar counts, you may be eligible for a fee waiver.

**8**    **Follow the rules.** Small claims cases often get thrown out because a plaintiff didn't file a case within a certain period of time or deliver the lawsuit documents to the defendant according to the rules of the court. Find out these rules—you can probably find them online or get a copy at the courthouse—and stick to them exactly.

**9**    **Your 15 minutes in court.** Without exception, small claims judges prefer hearing well-organized cases. Practice your presentation, making sure you succinctly cover the important points.

**10**    **One shot and one shot only.** If you sue and lose, you have no right to appeal. However, a defendant who loses may appeal.

## This TV Show Is Now in Session

A few things you might not know about those small claims court TV shows like *Judge Judy*, *Judge Joe Brown*, and *People's Court*:

- Many cases are pulled from actual small claims court dockets—the parties are invited on to the shows.

- The judges' decisions are based on established legal precedent.

- If you lose, you don't actually pay out of your own pocket. Most shows set up a fund and divide that sum based on the decision.

- Judge Wapner's father, an attorney, appeared frequently on the 1950s TV show *Divorce Court*.

# Is Golf Enough?

## Planning Your Retirement

Remember when you left home and started your first job? Retiring can be as big a transition, except more complicated. Planning your financial, social, vocational, and avocational needs now will help smooth the adjustment. It's never too early or too late to start—honest!

**TEN**
things you
should know
. . . . . . . . .

1 **What's the hurry?** Working part time or consulting can ease your transition to retirement. You may even enjoy your job again!

2 **How much will you need?** Traditionally, planners say that retirees will need approximately 80% of their working salary. However, it really depends on you—you may want to live it up! Calculate now your post-retirement income needs.

3 **Take a deep breath and add it up.** What will your sources of income be? Start with Social Security (it won't be eliminated, no matter what you hear). If you had a pension, add that, along with income from 401(k)s, IRAs, Roth IRAs, savings accounts (including CDs), and investment accounts. How does that compare to No. 2?

4 **Don't panic.** If you're behind in what you think you'll need, there are plenty of ways to adjust. Work longer, delay taking Social Security benefits (see No. 5), downsize or reverse mortgage your home, cut back on expenses, move to a less-expensive area (but see No. 6), even start a new business or career (one you've always wanted).

5 **Wait on Social Security.** If you retire early (between age 62 and your "full retirement age," which is between 65 and 67, depending on your year of birth), your Social Security checks are reduced forever.

6 **Dreaming of leaving winter behind?** We've all heard of people getting bored in their beach condo and moving back home—at great cost. Try leasing your house and renting elsewhere for a year before making a decision.

7 **"Can you make 50 copies?"**
Volunteering can expose you to new friends, provide fulfillment, and allow you to give back. But not every organization offers volunteers a meaningful experience. Before committing, meet the people and find out what you'd be doing. You didn't quit your job to do work you hate.

*If your pension plan was terminated or the company shut down, check with the Pension Benefit Guaranty.*

8 **Get out there.** Start a healthy lifestyle you can build on in retirement. Stop smoking, get regular checkups, and find an exercise routine that you actually enjoy (swimming? tennis? dancing?).

9 **Less is more.** "Retail therapy" provides comfort in a stressful working life. With more freedom, you may need less. Then, more frugal ways—such as taking up gourmet cooking instead of eating out—can feel like an opportunity rather than a restriction.

10 **Relationships count.** You already know this, right? Now's the time to live it. Mend fences. Don't be shy about calling people with whom you haven't talked in years—they'll be thrilled! If you're part of a couple, don't plan all your social outings as twosomes. Friends who are yours alone are essential.

### *I Guess He Really Loved His Work*

According to the *Guiness Book of World Records*, grave digger
Johann Heinrich Karl Thieme, sexton of Aldenburg,
Germany, dug 23,311 graves during a 50-year career.

### *Is your Social Security statement correct?*

If not, call Social Security so you don't miss benefits due
you. (800-772-1213; TTY 1-800-325-0778.)

# 401(k)s, IRAs, and Other Mysteries

48

## Retirement Plans

You've been carefully socking away the money for years, waiting, patiently waiting, until you can take it out to buy that vintage Airstream and travel the back roads. Before you withdraw, here are ten things you should know about retirement plans.

1 **Hands off my money!** Corporate retirement plans are exempt from greedy creditors, and the same is true for IRAs and Roth IRAs (in which case up to $1 million is exempt).

2 **Check, please!** Nearly half of American workers cash out their 401(k) savings when they change jobs instead of rolling it over into an IRA.

3 **It's not completely locked up.** You're not always penalized for taking money out of a 401(k) before age 59½. If you retire after age 55 and take a distribution of some or all of your 401(k) funds, there's no early distribution tax—though you still have to pay income taxes on the amount withdrawn.

4 **It goes the other way, too.** Just because you have passed age 59½ doesn't guarantee that you can take money out of your retirement plan. Many qualified plans do not permit distributions while you're still working.

5 **No penalty, but lots of paperwork.** At any age, you can start taking out payments based on your life expectancy or that of you and your beneficiary. (The IRS rules for doing this are fiendishly complex, though.)

**6** **What's a Roth 401(k)?** Contributions to traditional 401(k) plans are tax-deductible, but contributions to Roth 401(k) plans will not be. Instead, the tax benefits for Roth 401(k)s will come when you take distributions, which will be tax-free as long as you meet certain requirements.

**7** **Keep on saving.** Just because you are retired or semi-retired doesn't mean that you can't make tax-deductible contributions to retirement plans such as IRAs.

**8** **Consider your rollover.** When you leave a job, it might be to your advantage not to roll over all of your employer stock into an IRA. Once you do this, all future distributions from the IRA will be taxed at ordinary rates—not capital gains rates.

**9** **It's a hopeful bunch.** Sixty-four percent of U.S. workers do not expect their standard of living to decline in retirement.

**10** **Some dreamers in there, too.** Thirty-two percent of U.S. workers say they have not saved for their retirement.

Retirement Plans 48

## Retirement Planning: Best Websites

- **The 401k Help Center** (www.401khelpcenter.com) has the most up-to-date information on 401(k) trends and news.

- **AARP** (www.aarp.org) has a solid financial planning and retirement center with good IRA and 401(k) advice. Click "Money" on the home page.

- **Yahoo Retirement and Planning Center** (http://finance.yahoo.com/retirement) offers unbiased information on all things related to retirement planning and financing.

- **Social Security Online** (www.ssa.gov) has a lot of helpful retirement planning information as well guidance in calculating benefits.

# Say Hello to the New Generation

49

## Becoming a Grandparent

Grandparents-to-be look a lot different these days. If you are one, you're probably in better health, will live longer, and have more energy than your own grandparents did. But you'll likely share with them the anticipation they experienced about this new and exciting role. As eager as you may be to contribute your thoughts, experience, and energy to your grandchild's upbringing, there are a few things to keep in mind.

**TEN**
things you
should know

1 **A delicate balance.** Your kids may need your time and energy, your financial help, or your wisdom to step back and not overwhelm them. Let your children know help and support are available, but wait for the invite before barging in.

2 **When money helps.** Providing appropriate financial help without making your kids feel you are trying to control them isn't always easy. Paying for discrete, predetermined expenses such as family vacations, school fees, and medical costs is often the best way to help.

3 **Money for school.** Contributing to a "529 Savings Plan" allows you to set aside tax-free money specifically for college tuition. Roth IRAs provide another option. Or your kids may need money sooner to fund quality child care or private school fees if the public schools are poor.

4 **No responsibility, but no authority, either.** Your joyful new role includes getting to spoil your grandkids a bit. But remember, you're not in charge and you must respect your child's rules. Be sensitive about planning visits and letting the new family help define your role.

5 **"And I would know you from . . . ?"** Although developing a bond with your new grandchild is exciting, don't forget your child and his or her partner. A new grandchild offers an opportunity to enrich your relationships with your child as well.

6    **Just in case.** Make sure you have a parental consent form to obtain medical treatment for your grandchild when needed, such as during overnight visits without mom and dad.

7    **Record important family history.** Catalogue and label pictures and record important facts about your life and family heirlooms. Many years from now your grandkids will appreciate your thoughtfulness.

8    **Review your estate plan.** If you have already designated your kids as beneficiaries, you may be done. But if you are wealthy or wish to ensure a certain amount goes to your grandchildren, consider establishing a trust directly benefiting them.

9    **When the line blurs.** If you're raising your grandchild, you may be entitled to time off from work to care for him or her, as well as access to work-sponsored health insurance programs. Unless you have custody, however, there may be limits on your legal rights to visit with your grandchild, provide medical care, or control schooling.

10   **Take care of yourself.** Don't neglect your own financial health (you can borrow for college a lot easier than you can for retirement). Set the limits you want for child care if you live close by. And mind your health— being there for a grandchild's college graduation is one of the best gifts you can give.

## Call Me Zeyde or Fafi

Silly nicknames are one of the best things about being a grandparent. Here are common names for grandma and grandpa around the world:

- Dutch: Oma/Opa

- Flemish: Bomma/Bompa

- French: Grandmère/Grandpère

- German: Oma/Opa

- Italian: Nonna/Nonno

- Polish: Babunia/Dziadzio

- Russian: Babushka/Dedushka

- Spanish: Abuela/Abuelo

If you're looking for fun ideas for grandparents' names ("Butter-Butt," anyone?), check out www.namenerds .com/uucn/granny.

# Passing On Your Stuff

## Planning Your Estate

Everyone knows they should, but no one ever wants to do estate planning. Who wants to think about your ultimate demise? Knowing that some of your loved ones may dislike how you divvy things up can make for more anxiety. Even doing the minimum, however, will relieve your guilt now and save the people you care about a lot of headaches (and perhaps a lot of money, too).

**TEN**
things you
should know

• • • • • • • • • • ▶

1 **Writing a will is easy.** Really, it is. All you need is a good do-it-yourself book or software program. Put down whom you want to inherit what, sign it in front of witnesses, and you're done. It doesn't need to be filed anywhere; just tuck it away in a safe place.

2 **Cover your bases.** Much of your valuable property—retirement accounts, life insurance proceeds, jointly owned real estate or cars—probably won't pass through your will. Make sure you know who will inherit it.

3 **About your retirement plan.** Your spouse has an automatic legal right to inherit the money in your 401(k) plan (but can give it up in writing).

4 **It's your decision.** You don't have to leave anything to your children. You should at least list them in your will, though, so it's clear that you didn't inadvertently overlook any of them.

5 **A common misconception.** Recipients don't pay income tax on money they inherit. (One exception: money in tax-deferred retirement plans.)

6 **You sure hear a lot about taxes, though.** Additionally, you don't have to worry about federal estate tax unless you leave more money in your estate than 98% of the U.S. population does. If you think estate tax will be an issue for your family, see a lawyer—you can afford it.

**7** **Be specific.** You can save your family a lot of hassle and argument if you specify whom you want to have items with special sentimental value. Sometimes the bitterest fights are over items that don't seem valuable at all.

**8** **Smith & Sons? Jones & Daughters?** If you own a business, make plans for what should happen to it after you're gone.

**9** **What's the difference?** Most people don't need a living trust (a substitute for a will that lets your family skip probate court after your death) until they are older or seriously ill. Until then, a simple will is enough.

**10** **Don't forget the obvious (a lot of people do).** None of your estate planning documents or insurance policies will do a damn bit of good if your family can't find them after you're gone.

Planning Your Estate 50

# The Great Stork Derby

Canadian prankster (and lawyer) Charles Vance Millar, who died in 1926, had fun with his will, leaving antigambling and antialcohol advocates shares in breweries and racetracks. (Many of them accepted the gifts readily.)

The childless Millar is best known, however, for offering a cash gift to the woman who gave birth to the most children in the ten years following his death.

The province of Ontario tried but failed to invalidate the will on the grounds it went against public policy. So at the end of the ten years, the cash (more than $500,000) was divided among four Toronto women who each had nine children. Two other women with disputed claims to having birthed even more children were given $12,500 each.

# Catalog

## *Business*

Book with CD-ROM                    Prices subject to change

www.nolo.com • 800-728-3555

● Book with CD-ROM

| | | |
|---|---|---|
| Negotiate the Best Lease for Your Business | $24.99 | LESP |
| Nolo's Crash Course in Business Basics (5 Audio CDs) | $34.99 | ABBIZ |
| Nolo's Quick LLC | $29.99 | LLCQ |
| Nonprofit Meetings, Minutes & Records | $39.99 | NORM |
| Patent Savvy for Managers | $29.99 | PATM |
| The Performance Appraisal Handbook | $29.99 | PERF |
| The Progressive Discipline Handbook | $34.99 | SDHB |
| Small Business in Paradise | $19.99 | SPAR |
| The Small Business Start-Up Kit | $29.99 | SMBU |
| The Small Business Start-Up Kit for California | $29.99 | OPEN |
| Starting & Building a Nonprofit | $29.99 | SNON |
| Starting & Running a Successful Newsletter or Magazine | $29.99 | MAG |
| Tax Deductions for Professionals | $34.99 | DEPO |
| Tax Savvy for Small Business | $36.99 | SAVVY |
| Working for Yourself: Law & Taxes for Independent Contractors, Freelancers & Consultants | $39.99 | WAGE |
| The Work From Home Handbook | $19.99 | US-HOM |
| Working With Independent Contractors | $34.99 | HICI |
| Wow! I'm in Business | $21.99 | WHOO |
| Your Limited Liability Company: An Operating Manual | $49.99 | LOP |
| Your Rights in the Workplace | $29.99 | YRW |

Book with CD-ROM

## Consumer

## Estate Planning & Probate

Book with CD-ROM

## Family Matters

| | | |
|---|---|---|
| Always Dad: Being a Great Father During & After Divorce | $16.99 | DIFA |
| Building a Parenting Agreement That Works | $24.99 | CUST |
| The Complete IEP Guide | $34.99 | IEP |
| Divorce & Money | $34.99 | DIMO |
| Divorce Without Court | $29.99 | DWCT |
| Do Your Own California Adoption: Nolo's Guide for Stepparents & Domestic Partners | $34.99 | ADOP |
| Every Dog's Legal Guide: A Must-Have for Your Owner | $19.99 | DOG |
| Get It Together: Organize Your Records So Your Family Won't Have To | $24.99 | GET |
| The Guardianship Book for California | $34.99 | GB |
| A Judge's Guide to Divorce | $24.99 | JDIV |
| A Legal Guide for Lesbian & Gay Couples | $34.99 | LG |
| Living Together: A Legal Guide for Unmarried Couples | $34.99 | LTK |
| Nolo's Essential Guide to Divorce | $24.99 | NODV |
| Nolo's IEP Guide: Learning Disabilities | $29.99 | IELD |
| Parent Savvy | $19.99 | PRNT |
| Prenuptial Agreements: How to Write a Fair & Lasting Contract | $34.99 | PNUP |

Book with CD-ROM

www.nolo.com • 800-728-3555

## Going to Court

## Homeowners, Landlords & Tenancy

Book with CD-ROM

## Immigration

Book with CD-ROM

## Money Matters

## Intellectual Property

Book with CD-ROM

| | | |
|---|---|---|
| Legal Guide to Web & Software Development | $44.99 | SFT |
| Nolo's Patents for Beginners | $24.99 | QPAT |
| Patent, Copyright & Trademark | $39.99 | PCTM |
| Patent It Yourself | $49.99 | PAT |
| Patent Pending in 24 Hours | $34.99 | PEND |
| Patenting Art & Entertainment: New Strategies for Protecting Creative Ideas | $39.99 | PATAE |
| Profit From Your Idea | $34.99 | LICE |
| The Public Domain | $34.99 | PUBL |
| Trademark: Legal Care for Your Business & Product Name | $39.99 | TRD |
| What Every Inventor Needs to Know About Business & Taxes | $21.99 | ILAX |

## Seniors & Retirement

| | | |
|---|---|---|
| Get a Life: You Don't Need a Million to Retire Well | $24.99 | LIFE |
| Long-Term Care: How to Plan & Pay for It | $24.99 | ELD |
| Nolo's Essential Retirement Tax Guide | $24.99 | RTAX |
| Retire—and Start Your Own Business | $24.99 | BOSS |
| Retire Happy | $19.99 | US-RICH |
| Social Security, Medicare & Government Pensions | $29.99 | SOA |
| Work Less, Live More: The Way to Semi-Retirement | $17.99 | RECL |
| The Work Less, Live More Workbook | $19.99 | RECW |

Book with CD-ROM

## Software

**Call or check our website at www.nolo.com for special discounts on Software!**

| | | |
|---|---|---|
| LLC Maker—Windows | $69.95 | LLP1 |
| LeaseWriter Plus—Windows | $49.95 | LWDI |
| Patent Pending Now!—Windows | $119.99 | PP1 |
| PatentEase Deluxe 6.0—Windows | $259.00 | PEAS |
| Personal RecordKeeper 5—Windows | $35.97 | RKD5 |
| Quicken Legal Business Pro 2009—Windows | $79.99 | SBQB9 |
| Quicken WillMaker Plus 2009—Windows | $39.99 | WQP9 |

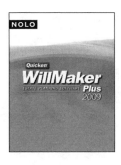